NATHAN'S FAMOUS HOT DOG COOKBOOK

HOT DOG COOKBOOK

by
MURRAY HANDWERKER

Illustrated by Fred Albert

GROSSET & DUNLAP
PUBLISHERS   NEW YORK

Murray Handwerker is president of Nathan's Famous of Coney Island and president of Nathan's Famous units in Oceanside, L.I., and Yonkers, N.Y. He is the son of Ida and Nathan Handwerker, the founders of Nathan's Famous, Inc. Nathan's is the world's largest and most renowned "Hot-Dog" mart. It sells eight million franks a year and was the first to use the noble frankfurter in gourmet food treats. It is a Mecca which attracts the greatest names in show business, government, sports, and the arts. Celebrities who have feasted on Nathan's hot dogs include Queen Mother Elizabeth of Great Britain, Mrs. Jacqueline Kennedy, Princess Grace of Monaco, Cary Grant, Barbra Streisand, former Presidents Eisenhower and Truman, Gov. Nelson Rockefeller, U.S. Senators Robert Kennedy and Jacob Javits, Mrs. Joseph P. Kennedy, Mayor John Lindsay, Zsa Zsa and Eva Gabor, Jimmy Durante, Danny Kaye, Red Skelton, Allen and Rossi, Jerry Lewis, Buddy Hackett, Ed Sullivan, Sandy Koufax, Ambassador Henry Cabot Lodge, Averell Harriman, Sammy Davis Jr., Joe Pepitone, Alan Arkin, Jack Carter, Phil Foster, Frank Sinatra, Milton Berle, Red Buttons, Alan King, Robert Goulet, Joey and Cindy Adams, and a host of others. "Nathan's" says *Time* Magazine, "is the spiritual home of the hot dog."

Mr. Handwerker is married to the former Dorothy Frankel and is the father of three sons who have been reared, of course, on hot dogs.

Introduction

The bride and groom emerged from the church in their wedding finery, braved the gauntlet of rice, and dashed into their brand-new convertible for the drive to the reception. As they purred along Surf Avenue in Coney Island, they approached Nathan's Famous and the bride said suddenly, "I know we're going to have a big meal at the reception, but I'm just dying for a Nathan's hot dog. Would you stop for a minute, darling?" And the groom answered, "We're not really dressed for this sort of thing, but it's a wonderful idea." So he jammed on the brakes, the two piled out and devoured a couple of hot dogs apiece. Then with a cheerful good-bye wave to fellow frankfurter munchers, they dashed back into the car and continued on to their wedding party—totally oblivious of the fact that the bride's long white gown was now decorated with two large mustard spots.

The fact that a bride in her expensive gown would delay getting to her wedding party just to stop off at Nathan's did not surprise our countermen because over the years they have become accustomed to seeing people from every strata of society and outfitted in every kind of dress descend on this Mecca of the Frankfurter World. To Nathan's have come Presidents and pipe-fitters, princesses and charwomen, sports stars and stenographers, UN delegates and steeplejacks, sultans of the desert and prospectors from Alaska, show business celebrities and extras with no speaking lines. They come by the millions, as varied in their backgrounds and interests as the traditional colors of the rainbow, but united in their passion for the wondrous wiener.

The majority come pouring out of the subway, where the conductors can be heard announcing, "Last stop, Coney Island!" But others come by family

car, taxi, chauffeured limousine, or even by boat. Then there are public officials like Gov. Nelson Rockefeller and Mayor John Lindsay who frequently come by helicopter. They arrive at a bustling, block-long landmark topped by huge, green-and-white signs and ringed by crowds that may be twelve deep along the sidewalk. Over the din of the crowd and the hissing of the steam griddles, they can hear the counter-men shouting, in the manner of the old-time barkers: "Step up! . . . Get 'em here! . . . Get 'em while they're hot!"

The signs proclaim that Nathan's Famous has gone "from a hot dog to an international habit." And so it has. Tourists from all over the world come to Nathan's and so do newly arrived immigrants who begin their integration into American customs by devouring the food snack that more than anything else symbolizes America. One of the better-known personalities who had an early introduction to the Nathan's hot dog after her arrival from abroad was Svetlana Alliluyeva, the daughter of Joseph Stalin.

From its main base in Coney Island or from its units in Oceanside, L.I., and Yonkers, N.Y., Nathan's air-expresses its products to hot dog and salami lovers the world over. These overseas Nathan's fans include U.S. servicemen stationed abroad, but they also include such world figures as Princess Grace of Monaco and Britain's Queen Mother Elizabeth, who first came into contact with a Nathan's hot dog at the memorable Hyde Park picnic of 1939, hosted for her and the late King George by President and Mrs. Franklin D. Roosevelt.

When Barbra Streisand held her closing-night party in London following her triumphant run in "Funny Girl," she had it catered by Nathan's from 3,000 miles away. When Father Frederic Gehring, the much-decorated "Padre of Guadalcanal," was un-able to attend ceremonies marking the twenty-fifth anniversary of the Guadalcanal battle, he sent a

Nathan's salami to the chairman of the ceremonies as a gastronomic gesture of good will. In Honolulu, the "Brooklyn Club of Hawaii" dines on Nathan's at its monthly luncheons. Guido Salmaggi, Italian Vice-Consul in Hawaii, says he has had Nathan's products follow him to all the far-flung diplomatic posts where he has been stationed. Movie mogul Jack Warner has Nathan's hot dogs sent to him regularly at his villa in Cannes, orders from Hollywood come almost daily and motion-picture stars like Alan Arkin, Maximillian Schell, George Segal, and Robert Goulet have their Nathan's packages dispatched to all the exotic places abroad where they make films on location.

Only the Soviet Union bars entry to Nathan's delicacies. Averell Harriman, Under-Secretary of State and former Governor of New York, ordered a Nathan's salami while in Moscow but Soviet customs stopped it at the border. The same thing happened to Raymonde Paul, an official of the International Federation of Women Lawyers. Said Mme. Paul, "The only explanation I can think of for this is that Soviet officials fear that if their people get a taste of a good American hot dog or salami, they'll all revolt!"

The frankfurter and its antecedent, the sausage, probably holds the all-time record for longevity as a popular food. The Babylonians feasted on sausages 3,500 years ago and both the ancient Greeks and the ancient Romans ate them with relish and probably flavored them with relish too, for all we know. In 1852, the butchers' guild in Frankfurt, Germany, produced the first sausage that was spiced, smoked, and packed with a casing. It was shaped like a dachshund because one of the butchers had a favorite pet dachshund.

When we speak of the modern hot dog, we refer to the frankfurter wrapped in a bun or roll. Its birth-

place was Coney Island and its inventor was Charles Feltman, who came to our Cote D'Azur for the masses from his native Frankfurt (hence the name "frankfurter"). Feltman sold pies from a little wagon which he drove up and down Coney Island's rustic trails. In 1867, two nearby inns began to serve hot sandwiches for lunch and Feltman became alarmed at the competition. He decided he'd better serve hot sandwiches, too.

Feltman's wagon was small and there was no room for elaborate cooking. Furthermore, he did not want to cook anything that would require long preparation or delicate seasoning. He finally hit on the idea of rigging up a small charcoal stove to boil frankfurters and then wrap them in toasted rolls.

The name of the customer who bought the first hot dog a little over one hundred years ago has been lost to posterity but he must have enjoyed it because he and others were soon clamoring "More, More!" The pie-man was able to open Feltman's Restaurant, featuring the hot dog as its pièce de resistance.

Shortly before World War I, my father, Nathan Handwerker, went to work for Feltman's as a roll-slicer and part-time delivery boy. Coney Island was then a plush resort area and an important entertainment center. Two of the most avid hot dog eaters along the beachfront were a singing waiter named Eddie Cantor and an accompanist named Jimmy Durante. Neither was in a state of affluence at the time and they resented the ten-cent price of the Feltman's frank. One day, they offered delivery boy Nathan some advice.

"Open your own place and sell a frankfurter at a price we can afford—a nickel," they counseled.

Dad took the Durante-Cantor suggestion to heart. By subsisting mostly on frankfurters, he had managed to accumulate a nest-egg of $300. In 1916, he opened his own little stand on Surf and Stillwell

Avenues and introduced the first five-cent red-hot. He used top-quality, low-fat meat in his frankfurters and provided extra succulence with a spice formula devised by his fiancée, Ida. Ida soon became his wife and partner. For many years, she worked full-time— and indeed overtime—at the stand and raised three children (myself included) in baskets behind the hot dog griddles.

Despite the high quality, which has always been a hallmark of Nathan's products, the first Nathan's red-hots found few takers. The society people at the resort just couldn't accept the fact that a five-cent frankfurter could be good. To change their minds, Dad hired a number of young men and outfitted them with white coats. They made a great show of eating the five-cent franks, so that people started to say, "Those frankfurters *must* be good. The doctors are eating them!"

Dad thus anticipated the "doctors commercials" on television by a few decades and the results were just as successful then as they were later to prove in the TV era. Crowds began to beat a path to the little stand. One woman, however, told Nathan that some people she sent to his place couldn't find it because it was lost among Coney's other attractions. "You have an oilcloth sign that says 'Hot Dogs'," she said, "but you don't say *whose* hot dogs. Your stand needs a name."

Nathan toyed with the idea of calling it "Handwerker's Hot Dogs" but that was too long for his sign. Providence in the form of "Tin Pan Alley" then provided a bright idea. At that time, a song called "Nathan, Nathan, Why You Waitin'?" became enormously popular. Dad decided that since Nathan was his real first name and the song was popularizing that name, he would call his place "Nathan's." (The "Famous" came a bit later.)

Hot dogs today are made as either all-beef products

or beef-pork combinations. Nathan's hot dogs are all-beef. The all-beef products are preferred by Consumers Union and nutritionists because they provide more protein and less fat than the beef-pork blend. Salt, spices, and sodium nitrate are added to the basic meat and then the mixture is chopped in a bowl-shaped machine. The blades revolve around so fast that crushed ice must be added to keep the meat from overheating. The chopped meat is then stuffed into a specially processed casing which becomes the frankfurter's outer coat. This "coat" preserves the food's mouth-watering juices.

The stuffed meat is placed in a linking machine which ties the casings at intervals which will yield the desired number of franks per pound. This converts each yard of the meat into seven linked frankfurters. These frankfurters are then cured in smokehouses and given a hot-water bath for 15 minutes. The process of smoking and bathing the franks brings out their flavor and provides them with their color.

Hot dogs may be boiled, of course, as well as grilled and broiled. However, we never boil frankfurters at Nathan's. We feel that the tastiest hot dog is one that is grilled and then put into a toasted roll. Hot dogs, incidentally, may be kept frozen for up to six months, with no loss in quality.

The long-run popularity of the hot dog is undoubtedly due to the fact that it is dependable enough to provide a succulent taste no matter who grills it. It may be prepared in a flavorsome manner by any man, woman or teen-ager, even though his or her credentials in the cooking profession are non-existent.

In this cookbook, I have provided recipes which take the hot dog far afield from its traditional role as a between-meals and an after-meals snack. You will find it in the role as Appetizer, as a Lunch Meal, a Main Dish, a Casserole, a feature of Continental cuisine, a soup element, a Barbecue Delight, and a Salad treat. By simply following the recipe directions,

you will find it as easy to prepare in its manifold new forms as it was in its basic position inside a roll. You will also discover that when consumed as Casserole, Main Dish, Continental special, or what have you, its delectable flavor will be enhanced, and not impaired. Thus, I ask you to prepare your taste buds for a series of toothsome delights and to approach your frankfurter-eating with that famous, all-American cry of pleasure, "Hot Dog!"

What They Say About
NATHAN'S HOT DOGS

Gov. Nelson Rockefeller—"No man can hope to get elected in New York State without being photographed eating hot dogs at Nathan's Famous."

Ambassador Henry Cabot Lodge—"I have always enjoyed a good hot dog and that's why I was so pleased by my visit to Nathan's. Mr. Nathan's hot dogs were extremely good . . . extremely tasty."

New York Mayor John Lindsay—"The hot dogs at Nathan's are always delicious. . . . As Mayor of New York, I take great pride in the fact that the world's largest and best-known frankfurter mart is in New York City."

Former Mayor Robert Wagner—"The Nathan's hot dog is the best you can eat anywhere."

Mrs. Rose Kennedy—"When John was campaigning for the Presidency, he didn't have time to visit Nathan's so I went for him. The hot dogs were wonderful and I took several packages back for John because I knew how much he would enjoy them."

Senator Robert Kennedy—"The Nathan's hot dog is one of New York's great institutions."

Contents

Soups and Chowders

4 hot dogs
   1 *quart boiling water*
   1 *cup large dry lima beans*
   1 *teaspoon salt*
   5 *beef bouillon cubes*
   5 *cups boiling water*
   1 *(10½ ounce) can Italian peeled tomatoes*
   6 *carrots, cut into quarters*
   ½ *cup frozen green beans, thawed*
   2 *ribs celery, sliced*
   3 *onions, sliced thin*
   ½ *teaspoon marjoram*
   1 *teaspoon sage*
     Salt and pepper to taste
   ¼ *teaspoon seasoned salt*

Hot Dog Vegetable Soup

Stir rinsed lima beans into the quart of boiling water, keeping it at the boil. Cover and simmer for 1 hour, adding 1 teaspoon of salt during the last 20 minutes. Add more water if needed. Add bouillon cubes dissolved in 5 cups of boiling water. Stir in the tomatoes, carrots, green beans, celery and onions. Simmer, uncovered, until the vegetables are tender, about 25 minutes. Cut the hot dogs in half lengthwise and add with the remaining ingredients. Heat to piping hot and serve with crackers.

Serves 4 to 6.

Hot Dog Bean Chowder

4 hot dogs
  2 *carrots, diced*
  2 *tablespoons butter or margarine, melted*
  2 *tablespoons onion, minced*
  2 *tablespoons green pepper, minced*
  2 *tablespoons flour*
    Salt and pepper to taste
  1 *cup milk*
  1 *(1 pound) can baked beans in tomato sauce*

Cook the carrots in 1 inch of boiling salted water until tender. Drain, reserving liquid. In the melted butter sauté the onion and green pepper. Add enough water to carrot liquid to make 1 cup. Combine this with milk. Stir into the onion-pepper-flour mixture in the skillet. Stirring constantly, heat until thickened. Add carrots, beans and hot dogs, chopped fine. Heat through. *Serves 4.*

Hot Dog Corn Chowder

4 hot dogs
  1 *onion, minced*
  2 *ribs celery, chopped*
  ¼ *cup green pepper, chopped*
  ¼ *cup butter or margarine*
  2 *small potatoes, peeled and diced*
  2 *cups water*
  1 *teaspoon salt*
  ½ *bay leaf, crumbled*
  ½ *teaspoon thyme*
  3 *cups cut fresh corn*
  3 *tablespoons flour*
  ½ *cup cold milk*
 1½ *cups hot milk*

Sauté the onion, celery and green pepper in the butter. Add potatoes, water, salt, bay leaf, thyme and hot dogs, cut into ½-inch slices. Cover and simmer until potatoes are almost tender. Add corn and simmer another 5 minutes. Blend flour and cold milk into a smooth paste. Add—a little at a time—to the vegetable mixture, stirring constantly. Simmer another 5 minutes, and blend in the hot milk.

Serves 4.

Hot Dog Zucchini Soup

8 hot dogs
  2½ *cups beef broth*
  1¼ *cups water*
  2 *cloves garlic, minced*
  2 *tablespoons butter or margarine*
  1½ *teaspoons basil, crushed*
  1 *teaspoon monosodium glutamate*
  4 *carrots, sliced into julienne strips*
  1 *large onion, minced*
    Salt and pepper to taste
  1 *(1 pound) zucchini squash, cut into ¼ inch slices*
  2 *tomatoes, peeled and cut into eighths*
  1 *teaspoon sugar*

In a large sauce pan, mix together all the ingredients except the hot dogs, cut into quarters, zucchini, tomatoes and sugar. Cover and simmer 20 minutes. Add remaining ingredients. Bring to a boil. Cover and allow to simmer another 10 minutes. *Serves 6.*

Quick and Easy Hot Dog Vegetable Soup

2 hot dogs
  1 *tablespoon butter or margarine, melted*
  1 *package dry vegetable soup mix*

Lightly brown the hot dogs, cut into ½-inch slices, in melted butter. Add the contents of the soup package with the amount of water specified in the package directions. Cook as directed. Serve with crackers. *Serves 3 to 4.*

Hot Dog Pea Soup

3 hot dogs
2 (10½ ounce) cans condensed pea soup
2 ribs celery, chopped fine
1 teaspoon onion, minced

Prepare soup according to directions on can. While it simmers, add the celery, onion and hot dogs, cut into ½-inch slices. Simmer another 10 minutes.

Serves 4.

Quick and Easy Hot Dog Potato Soup

4 hot dogs
4 slices bacon, cut into tiny pieces
1 onion, chopped
1½ cups chicken broth
1 teaspoon celery salt
1 (4 serving) package of instant mashed potatoes
1 (8 ounce) can whole kernel corn
1⅔ cups milk
Salt and pepper to taste

Cook the bacon and hot dogs cut into ½-inch slices in a heavy saucepan until the bacon is crisp. Remove bacon and reserve. Spoon off all but 2 tablespoons of the fat. Add the onion and cook over low heat until the onion is tender. Add the broth and celery salt. Heat to boiling. Remove from heat. Stir the package of instant mashed potatoes and the milk into the soup. Stir in the corn, including its liquid. Heat through. Add salt, pepper and crumbled bacon.

Serves 4 to 6.

Main Dishes

6 hot dogs
   2 *tablespoons salad oil*
   ½ *small onion, minced*
   ¼ *teaspoon thyme*
   1 *teaspoon seasoned salt*
   2 *cups canned lima beans*
   1 *teaspoon vinegar*
   ¼ *cup catsup*

Quick Lima Skillet

Sauté the onion in the oil until tender. Add the hot dogs, cut into diagonal slices, and brown very lightly. Stir in the other ingredients. Simmer until hot through, about five minutes, and serve.

Serves 4.

---

8 hot dogs
   4 *tablespoons butter or margarine, melted*
  10 *small onions, sliced*
   1 *teaspoon soy sauce*
   5 *green peppers, sliced into strips*
    Pepper, to taste

Peppered Hot Dogs

Sauté the onions and green peppers in the melted butter or margarine in a large skillet. Add the hot dogs, cut crosswise into ½-inch slices, and soy sauce. Stir to mix thoroughly. Sprinkle the pepper over all. Stir again. Cover the skillet and allow to simmer for 30 minutes, stirring occasionally. *Serves 4.*

9

Sauerkraut Creole

8 hot dogs
 3 *tablespoons butter or margarine, melted*
 1 *onion, chopped*
 1 *green pepper, chopped*
 1 *pound undrained sauerkraut*
 2 *cups canned tomato sauce*
   Salt and pepper to taste

Sauté the onion and pepper in the melted butter or margarine until tender. Add the sauerkraut, tomato sauce and salt and pepper. Simmer for 10 minutes. Then cut the hot dogs crosswise into ½-inch slices, add to sauerkraut and simmer for another 10 minutes.   *Serves 4.*

Curried Hot Dogs

8 hot dogs
 2 *small onions, chopped*
 1 *cored apple, chopped*
 3 *tablespoons butter or margarine, melted*
 1 *tablespoon curry powder*
 1 *tablespoon flour*
 1 *cup boiling water*
 2 *bouillon cubes*

Sauté the onions, apple and hot dogs, cut crosswise into 1-inch slices, in the butter until onions are transparent. Dissolve bouillon cubes in boiling water in a saucepan. Combine the curry powder and flour, and stir this mixture carefully into the bouillon, stirring constantly to blend. Bring to a boil and add the·hot dog mixture. Cover and simmer until hot dogs are heated through, about 10 minutes. Serve with rice.
                                    Serves 4.

8 hot dogs
>   5 *cups boiling water*
>   1 *cup canned Italian peeled tomatoes*
> 1½ *cups uncooked elbow macaroni*
>   *Salt and pepper to taste*
>   ¼ *pound butter or margarine*
>   ½ *cup cheese, grated*

**Hot Dogs-
n-Macaroni**

Combine boiling water and canned tomatoes in a large skillet and bring to a boil. Stir in the macaroni. Cook 15 minutes, stirring frequently. Dice the hot dogs, add to macaroni and season with salt and pepper. Cook for another 10 minutes, continuing to stir to prevent sticking. Turn into a serving dish. Top with butter and grated cheese.   *Serves 4 to 6.*

---

4 hot dogs
>   3 *tablespoons salad oil*
>   2 *small onions, minced*
>   1 *cup mushrooms, sliced*
>   1 *tablespoon flour*
> 1½ *cups tomato juice*
>   1 *cup water*
>   1 *tablespoon Worcestershire sauce*
>   *Salt and pepper to taste*
>   2 *tablespoons parsley, chopped*
>   ¼ *cup green pepper, minced*
>   ½ *pound spaghetti*
>   *Parmesan cheese*

**Spaghetti
and
Hot Dogs**

Chop the hot dogs. Sauté the onions and mushrooms in the oil. Stir in the flour and chopped hot dogs. Add tomato juice, water, Worcestershire sauce, salt and pepper. Simmer for 25 minutes. Add the chopped parsley and green pepper. Simmer for another 5 minutes. Meanwhile cook the spaghetti according to package directions. Mix spaghetti with sauce. Serve with Parmesan cheese.   *Serves 4.*

Spaghetti with Hot Dog Sauce

3 hot dogs
  2 *tablespoons butter or margarine, melted*
  1 *scallion, minced*
  2 *cans condensed tomato soup*
  2 *teaspoons sugar*
  ½ *pound hot, buttered spaghetti*
  4 *teaspoons Parmesan cheese, grated*

Sauté the hot dogs, chopped, and scallion in the melted butter. Stir in the undiluted soup and sugar. After preparing spaghetti according to package directions, top it with the hot dog sauce. Sprinkle with grated cheese and serve.   *Serves 4.*

Hot Dog Stuffed Peppers

8 hot dogs
     4 *large green peppers*
  1¼ *teaspoon salt*
     ¼ *cup onions, minced*
     2 *ribs of celery, minced*
     1 *teaspoon salt*
     ¼ *cup green pepper, minced*
     1 *egg, unbeaten*
     ½ *cup light cream*
  2½ *cups canned Italian tomatoes*
     1 *small onion, minced*
     ½ *teaspoon salt*
     1 *tablespoon sugar*
     ¼ *teaspoon cinnamon*
     1 *tablespoon flour*
     ¼ *cup cold water*

Wash peppers, cut strip from top and remove seeds. Boil peppers in water with 1¼ teaspoon salt for five minutes. Drain. Grind hot dogs. Combine hot dogs, onions, celery, salt, minced peppers, egg and cream. Stuff peppers with hot dog mixture. Place peppers in a baking dish. Combine tomatoes and onions in a saucepan. Add ½ teaspoon salt, sugar and cinnamon. Simmer 10 minutes. Strain, saving liquid. Combine flour and cold water, and add to strained liquid; cook until thickened, stirring constantly. Add tomato pulp, and heat through. Pour over peppers. Bake 50 minutes in a 350° oven.   *Serves 4.*

Hot Dog Cabbage Carousel

8 hot dogs
1 *head white cabbage, shredded*
2 *tablespoons butter or margarine, melted*
1 *small onion, minced*
2 *tablespoons vinegar*

Cook the shredded cabbage in butter until tender—about 10 minutes—stirring constantly to avoid burning. When the cabbage is slightly browned, add the onion and cook another minute. Add the vinegar. Turn onto a hot oval platter, pressing the cabbage toward the center to make room for a ring of hot dogs. Meanwhile, grill the hot dogs in a skillet until slightly browned. Arrange the hot dogs in a circle around the cabbage.   *Serves 4.*

Duchess Hot Dogs

12 hot dogs
1 *(12-serving) package instant mashed potatoes*
½ *teaspoon sweet basil*
Salt and pepper to taste
½ *teaspoon thyme*
Paprika

Prepare the instant mashed potatoes according to the package directions, blending in the basil, thyme and salt and pepper. Force through a pastry tube into split hot dogs. Sprinkle with paprika and brown under broiler.   *Serves 6.*

**Hot Dogs
and Lima
Beans**

8 hot dogs
  2 *tablespoons butter*
  2 *tablespoons flour*
1½ *cups milk*
 ¼ *teaspoon salt*
 ¼ *teaspoon white pepper*
 ¾ *cup sharp Cheddar cheese, grated*
2½ *cups baby lima beans, cooked*

Melt butter and blend in flour. Add milk and cook, stirring constantly, until thickened. Season with salt and pepper. Add cheese and stir until melted. Add hot dogs, cut into ½-inch slices, and lima beans. Heat in the top of a double boiler until piping hot.
Serves 4.

**Hot Dog
Stuffed
Cabbage**

7 hot dogs
  4 *outer leaves from a cabbage*
 ½ *cup crumbled corn flakes*
 ½ *small onion, minced*
 ¼ *teaspoon celery seeds*
   Salt and pepper, to taste
  2 *teaspoons sugar*
 ½ *teaspoon Worcestershire sauce*
  1 *egg, well-beaten*
  1 *tablespoon butter or margarine, melted*
  1 *(1-pound) can solid pack tomatoes*
 ¼ *cup Cheddar cheese, grated*

Mince 4 hot dogs; cut remaining 3 hot dogs crosswise in half and set aside. Simmer the cabbage leaves in water in a covered pot for 5 minutes; drain and spread out for filling. Combine the minced hot dogs with the crumbled corn flakes, onion, celery seeds and salt and pepper. Spoon one-fourth of this mixture onto the center of each cabbage leaf. Roll up each cabbage leaf, folding the ends toward the center. Secure the ends with toothpicks. Place the stuffed cabbage rolls in a skillet with the butter. Add drained tomatoes and ¼ cup of the tomato liquid. Stir in the sugar. Cover and simmer for 25 minutes. Add the sliced hot dogs. Sprinkle with grated cheese. Simmer another 10 minutes. Remove toothpicks, and serve piping hot. *Serves 4.*

Hot Dog Island Stew

6 hot dogs
  1 *onion*
  1 *rib celery, minced*
  3 *tablespoons butter or margarine, melted*
  1 *cup tomato catsup*
  3 *cups water*
  1 *teaspoon steak sauce*
 ¼ *cup cold water*
   Salt and pepper to taste
  4 *medium potatoes, cubed*
  3 *cooked carrots, sliced into coins*
  1 *tablespoon parsley, minced*
  2 *tablespoons flour*
  2 *cups biscuit mix*

Cut the hot dogs into ½-inch slices. Sauté them with the onions and celery in the butter in a large pan. When the hot dogs are lightly browned, add the catsup, water, steak sauce and salt and pepper. Bring to a boil and add the potatoes, carrots and parsley. Cover the pan, and allow to simmer about 30 minutes or until the carrots and potatoes are tender. Combine the flour and cold water, and add this to mixture in pan. Stirring constantly, simmer another 5 minutes or until mixture thickens. Follow package instructions to make dumplings from biscuit mix. By the spoonful, drop the dumplings onto the hot stew. Cover, and cook an additional 10 minutes. *Serves 6 to 8.*

Squash
Lyonnaise
with
Hot Dogs

6 hot dogs
  1 *pound zucchini*
  1 *pound yellow squash*
  1 *onion, sliced thin*
  ¼ *cup butter or margarine, melted*

Cook the zucchini and yellow squash until tender, and set aside. Cut hot dogs in half crosswise. Sauté the onion in the melted butter. Add the hot dog halves and brown lightly. Add the zucchini and yellow squash and heat.   *Serves 4.*

Cornfurters

6 hot dogs
  1 *small onion, chopped*
  ¼ *cup green pepper, chopped*
  1 *tablespoon butter or margarine, melted*
  1 *(1 pound) can creamed corn*

Cut the hot dogs into ½-inch slices, then brown the slices, onion and green pepper in the butter. Add the corn, and heat. Serve piping hot.   *Serves 6.*

Hot Dog
Pan
Barbecue

8 hot dogs
  2 *tablespoons butter or margarine, melted*
  1 *onion, minced*
  1 *teaspoon chili powder*
  1 *can condensed tomato soup*
  ½ *cup water*

Slash hot dogs diagonally every inch. Brown them in the melted butter. Add onion and chili powder, and sauté 1 minute. Stir in the soup and water. Simmer for 5 minutes, stirring occasionally.
    Serves 4 to 6.

12 hot dogs
   2 *tablespoons butter or margarine, melted*
  ½ *cup uncooked rice*
   1 *onion, chopped*
   2 *cups canned peeled tomatoes*
   1 *rib celery, minced*
     Salt and pepper to taste
   2 *teaspoons sugar*
   1 *bay leaf*

**Hot Dog
Rice
Island**

Sauté the rice in the melted butter. When the rice is yellow, add the onion and continue to sauté for three minutes. Add the tomatoes, celery, salt and pepper, sugar and bay leaf. Mix together gently, and cover. Allow to simmer about 20 minutes or until the rice is tender. Meanwhile, grill the hot dogs in a skillet until lightly browned. Spoon the tomato-rice mixture in the center of a large platter. Arrange the hot dogs around the "island" of rice.   *Serves 6.*

----

8 hot dogs
   2 *tablespoons butter or margarine, melted*
   1 *onion, sliced very thin*
   1 *small green pepper, cut into thin strips*
   3 *ribs celery, sliced thin*
 2½ *cups canned tomatoes*
   1 *(8-ounce) can tomato sauce*
   2 *teaspoons chili powder*
   1 *teaspoon sugar*
     Salt and pepper to taste

**Hot Dogs
Louisiana**

Sauté the onion, green pepper and celery in the melted butter until the vegetables are tender, about 5 minutes. Add the tomatoes, tomato sauce, chili powder, sugar and salt and pepper. Mix together thoroughly. Simmer, uncovered, for 10 minutes. Add the hot dogs, cut into thirds, and heat thoroughly.   *Serves 6 to 8.*

**Hot Dog
Shortcake**

8 hot dogs
2 *cups chicken broth*
1 *green pepper, chopped*
½ *cup canned mushrooms*
4 *tablespoons butter or margarine, melted*
5 *tablespoons flour*
  Salt and pepper to taste
¼ *teaspoon paprika*
8 *shortcake biscuits or patty shells*

Cut the hot dogs into 1-inch slices. Heat the slices
in the chicken broth. Add the green pepper, mushrooms and mushroom liquid. Bring to a boil, and
allow to simmer for 3 minutes. Meanwhile, blend
the flour, salt and pepper and paprika into the
melted butter in a heavy skillet. Stir in the hot dog
mixture. Cook until slightly thickened, stirring constantly. Spoon the mixture over split shortcake biscuits or patty shells and serve immediately.

Serves 4.

**Hot Dogs
and
Dumplings**

8 hot dogs
¼ *cup flour*
2 (*1 pound*) *cans stewed tomatoes*
½ *cup pitted ripe olives sliced*
  Salt and pepper to taste
1 *can refrigerated biscuits*
8 *ounces cheese, shredded*

Mix flour, tomatoes and olives together in a skillet.
Heat to boiling, stirring constantly. Add the hot
dogs, halved lengthwise, and heat thoroughly. Using
kitchen scissors, cut the biscuits into quarters. Drop
the biscuit quarters into the simmering tomato-hot
dog mixture. Sprinkle with the shredded cheese.
Cover. Simmer gently for 30 minutes. *Serves 4 to 6.*

12 hot dogs
   3½ *tablespoons olive oil*
    2 *onions, chopped*
    2 *ribs celery, chopped*
   ¼ *teaspoon thyme*
      Crushed red pepper to taste
    1 *(2 pound) can Italian peeled tomatoes*
    2 *tablespoons tomato paste*
    1 *teaspoon fennel seeds*
    1 *can sliced mushrooms, drained*
      Salt and pepper to taste

Hot Dogs with Fennel

Heat the olive oil in a heavy skillet. Add onion, celery, thyme and red pepper. Cook slowly until onions are tender. Add hot dogs, cut into ½-inch slices, tomatoes, tomato paste and fennel seeds. Simmer for 45 minutes. Add mushrooms and salt and pepper. Simmer another 15 minutes. Serve piping hot.
Serves 4 to 6.

---

8 hot dogs
   2 *tablespoons chicken fat*
   1 *onion, chopped*
   ¼ *cup wine vinegar*
   ¼ *cup water*
   1 *tablespoon prepared mustard*
   ¾ *cup beef bouillon, thickened with flour*
   2 *tablespoons tomato catsup*
   ½ *cup pickle relish*

Hot Dogs-n-Gravy

Melt the chicken fat. Add the hot dogs and onion and sauté until the onion is tender. Stir in the vinegar, water and mustard. Cover and simmer for 5 minutes. Remove the hot dogs. Stir in the beef bouillon that has been thickened with flour. Add the catsup and pickle relish. Stir until well heated. Add the hot dogs. Allow to simmer another minute. Serve with boiled or mashed potatoes. *Serves 4 to 6.*

Caraway-
kraut
Hot Dogs

8 hot dogs
  2 *tart apples, pared, cored and sliced*
  1 *(1 pound) can sauerkraut*
  1 *tablespoon caraway seeds*
  1 *tablespoon vinegar*

Combine all ingredients except hot dogs. Bring to a boil, then simmer for 5 minutes. Place hot dogs on top. Cover pan, bring to a boil and simmer for 10 minutes.   *Serves 4 to 6.*

Hot Dog
Ragout

8 hot dogs
  1 *onion, sliced thin*
  3 *tablespoons butter or margarine, melted*
  1 *cup tomato catsup*
  3 *cups water*
  2 *teaspoons Worcestershire sauce*
    Salt and pepper to taste
  4 *potatoes, peeled and cubed*
  4 *carrots, sliced thin*
  1 *small can peas, drained*
  2 *tablespoons parsley, minced*

Sauté the onion in the melted butter. Combine the catsup, water, Worcestershire sauce and salt and pepper, and stir this mixture into the onion. Add the potatoes and carrots and cover. Cook until vegetables are tender. Cut hot dogs into 1-inch slices, add to the other ingredients and allow to simmer for 20 minutes. Stir in the peas and simmer until they are hot. Turn into a serving dish. Sprinkle with parsley.   *Serves 4 to 6.*

8 hot dogs
   3 *tablespoons butter or margarine, melted*
   1 *cup bottled barbecue sauce*
   1 *can small onions, drained*
   ½ *pound wide egg noodles*

**Hot Dogs
and
Onions**

Cut 4 hot dogs in halves crosswise. Sauté the whole hot dogs and the halved hot dogs in the melted butter. Add the barbecue sauce and the onions and allow to simmer for a few minutes. Meanwhile, cook the noodles according to the directions on the package. Place noodles on a large oval platter. Top with the hot dog and onion mixture. *Serves 4 to 6.*

---

10 hot dogs
   ¼ *cup granulated brown sugar*
   ¼ *cup cornstarch*
   ¼ *cup vinegar*
   ¼ *cup orange marmalade*
   1 *cup pineapple juice*
   1 *(13½ ounce) can pineapple tidbits, with juice*
   ½ *cup seeded and split green grapes*
  10 *Maraschino cherries*
   1 *cup drained Mandarin orange sections*
   ½ *cup Cointreau*

**Hot Dog
Flambé**

Mix together the granulated brown sugar and the cornstarch. Set aside. Mix together the vinegar, orange marmalade, pineapple juice and undrained pineapple tidbits in a chafing dish. Stir in the sugar-cornstarch mixture, and continue to stir while heating until thickened. Add the hot dogs, cut diagonally into quarters, grapes, cherries and orange sections. Bring the chafing dish to the table, along with the Cointreau. Continue to heat. Pour the Cointreau over all. Ignite and serve with a flourish. *Serves 6.*

Top Hats   8 hot dogs
         2 *cups sauerkraut*
         1 *tablespoon flour*
         1¼ *teaspoon sage*
         8 *slices rye bread, buttered*
         2 *teaspoons prepared mustard*

Drain the sauerkraut, reserving ½ cup juice. Mix this
reserved juice with the flour and sage; stir this mixture into the sauerkraut. Heat, stirring constantly,
until it thickens. Cut diagonal slits into hot dogs,
going almost through. Broil the hot dogs until they
are hot. As they broil, they will curl into circles. Place
curled hot dog circle on each slice of bread, making
sure ends touch to make full circle. Top each circle
with a mound of the sauerkraut mixture. Top each
mound with ½ teaspoon mustard.   *Serves 8.*

Hot Dog   6 hot dogs
Omelet   1 *onion, chopped*
         1 *green pepper, sliced thin*
         2 *tablespoons butter or margarine*
         8 *eggs, beaten*
         2 *tablespoons milk*
         ½ *teaspoon orégano*
         Salt and pepper, to taste

Sauté the onion, green pepper and hot dogs, sliced
thin, in the butter or margarine in a large heavy
skillet. Mix eggs with milk, orégano and salt and
pepper. Pour egg mixture into skillet. Stirring gently,
cook over a low fire until the eggs attain the desired
consistency.   *Serves 4.*

Casseroles

8 hot dogs
1 (½ pound) package of elbow macaroni, cooked and buttered
2 onions, chopped
4 ribs celery, sliced thin
¼ cup butter or margarine, melted
2 tablespoons flour
Salt and pepper to taste
2½ cups milk
1 tablespoon prepared mustard
2 cups American cheese, shredded

Macaroni Hot Dog Casserole

Sauté the onion and celery in the melted butter. Stir in the flour, salt and pepper. Add the milk and continue to stir until thickened. Add mustard and 1½ cups of the cheese and continue to stir until the cheese melts. Combine the sauce with the cooked macaroni and all but ¾ cup of hot dogs, cut diagonally into ½-inch slices. Pour into a baking dish and garnish with remaining hot dog slices. Sprinkle with the remaining cheese. Bake in a 350° oven until bubbly around the edges.   *Serves 4 to 6.*

Hot Dog Tarts

8 hot dogs
1 (*10½ ounce*) *can condensed bean and bacon soup*
1¼ *cups water*
2 *tablespoons prepared mustard*
1 *onion, chopped*
1 *green pepper, chopped*
2 *ribs celery, chopped*
1 *can refrigerated biscuits*

Mix the condensed soup and the water together in a large saucepan. Stir in the prepared mustard, onion, green pepper, celery and hot dogs, cut into 1-inch slices. Simmer gently for 5 minutes. Using 8 individual casseroles that hold about 1½ cups each, divide the soup and hot dog mixture evenly among them. Top each casserole with a biscuit, and bake in a 375° oven until the biscuits are brown, about 20 minutes.   *Serves 8.*

Hot Dogs New England

6 hot dogs
2 (*1 pound*) *cans pork and beans*
2 *tablespoons Worcestershire sauce*
½ *teaspoon Tabasco sauce*
2 *tablespoons brown sugar*
2 *tablespoons molasses*
Juice ½ lemon
¼ *teaspoon thyme*
2 *large onions*

Cut hot dogs in half lengthwise. Mix baked beans with Worcestershire sauce, Tabasco sauce, brown sugar, molasses, lemon juice and thyme. Slice onions and separate into rings. Mix lightly with the beans. Bake, covered, in a 375° oven for ½ hour. Place hot dog halves on top of beans for another ½ hour, uncovered, in the oven. Serve very hot with tomato wedges and buttered water crackers.   *Serves 4.*

8 hot dogs
  1 (*1 pound*) *can beans in tomato sauce*
  ¼ *teaspoon dry mustard*
  ½ *teaspoon Worcestershire sauce*
  ¼ *teaspoon brown sugar*
  ½ *cup Cheddar cheese, grated*

**Cheesy
Hot Dogs
and Beans**

Combine the beans, mustard, Worcestershire sauce
and brown sugar in a casserole. Arrange hot dogs on
top, pressing each hot dog slightly into the bean
mixture. Sprinkle with grated cheese. Bake for 20
minutes in a 350° oven. *Serves 4.*

---

8 hot dogs
  1 *tablespoon butter or margarine*
  1 *onion, diced*
  2 *ribs celery, diced*
  1 *small green pepper, diced*
  2½ *cups canned tomatoes*
    Thyme and orégano to taste
    Salt and pepper to taste
    Pinch of sugar
  1 *package corn bread mix*

**Dixie Dog
Casserole**

Melt the butter in a saucepan. Add the onion, celery and green pepper. Sauté until tender. Cut hot
dogs into thirds, add all ingredients except the corn
bread mix. Simmer for 10 minutes. Pour this mixture into a large casserole. Prepare corn bread mix
according to directions on package. Spread the batter over the casserole top. Bake for 25 minutes—or
until the corn bread turns golden brown—in a 425°
oven. *Serves 6.*

Creamed Vegetable Casserole

8 hot dogs
  4 *carrots, cooked and cut diagonally into 1-inch chunks*
 12 *small onions, cooked*
  1 *(8 ounce) can peas, drained*
  3 *tablespoons flour*
 ⅛ *pound butter or margarine, melted*
  1 *cup milk*
  1 *cup cream*
 ½ *teaspoon sweet basil*
 ½ *teaspoon sugar*
    Salt and white pepper to taste
  1 *package refrigerated biscuits*

Combine carrots, onions and peas and set aside. In a separate skillet, stir the flour into the melted butter and cook 2 minutes. Add the milk, cream, sweet basil, sugar, salt and pepper. Stir until thickened. Add the combined vegetables to the cream sauce. Pour the mixture into an extra large casserole. Cut each hot dog in half crosswise and wrap in a biscuit. Stand these rolls around the edges of the casserole, dipping slightly into the vegetable combination. Bake in a 450° oven until biscuits are done, about 15 minutes.   *Serves 6.*

Hot Dog Vegetable Casserole

8 hot dogs
  1 *(8 ounce) can kernel corn, drained*
  1 *(8 ounce) can peas, drained*
  2 *(10½ ounce) cans condensed tomato soup*
  1 *package corn bread mix*

Place hot dogs, cut into 1-inch slices, in a square baking dish. Spoon the drained corn and peas over the hot dog slices. Pour tomato soup evenly over all. Place in a 425° oven to heat while preparing the corn bread mix according to package directions.

Spread over the top of the soup mixture. Bake about 25 minutes, until the corn bread is crusty and golden brown.   *Serves 4.*

---

8 hot dogs
   3 *cups canned sauerkraut, rinsed and drained*
    Pepper to taste
   1 *tablespoon brown sugar*
   1 *cup canned tomato sauce*

Hot Dog Sauerkraut Casserole

Place the sauerkraut in a 1½-quart casserole. Sprinkle with pepper and brown sugar. Top with tomato sauce, poured evenly over all. Cut each hot dog into three pieces. Press pieces into sauerkraut. Cover the casserole. Bake in a 400° oven for 15 minutes. Uncover and bake an additional 15 minutes. Serve in casserole.   *Serves 4.*

---

8 hot dogs
   1 *onion, chopped*
   1 *green pepper, chopped*
  ½ *cup celery, chopped*
   3 *tablespoons butter or margarine, melted*
 2½ *tablespoons flour*
 1¼ *cups milk*
    Salt and pepper to taste
   2 *cups mashed potatoes*

Hot Dog Potato Casserole

Cut the hot dogs into ½-inch slices. Brown them in butter, along with the onion, green pepper and celery. Very carefully blend in the flour. Do not let the flour burn. Blend in the milk. Allow to simmer, stirring constantly, until thickened. Add the salt and pepper. Turn the mixture into a baking dish. Top with mashed potatoes as for a shepherd's pie. Bake for 30 minutes in a 350° oven.   *Serves 4 to 6.*

Potato Hot Dog Casserole

6 hot dogs
1 (12 ounce). package frozen potato patties
    Salt and pepper to taste
1 onion, minced
¾ cup milk
1 tablespoon butter or margarine

In a 1½-quart greased casserole, arrange layers of potato patties, sliced hot dogs and onion. Sprinkle with salt and pepper. Pour milk over all, and dot with butter. Cover and bake in a 350° oven until potatoes are tender, about an hour. Stir with a fork several times while baking, to break up patties.

Serves 4.

Creamed Hot Dog Casserole

8 hot dogs
1 onion, sliced
1 green pepper, cut into slivers
3 tablespoons salad oil
2 pimientos, diced
2 (8 ounce) cans whole kernel corn, drained
    Salt and pepper to taste
1 can undiluted condensed cream of celery soup
1 pimiento, cut into strips for garnish

Slowly cook the onion, green pepper and 7 hot dogs, cut into 1-inch slices, in the oil for about 5 minutes. Stir in the diced pimientos, corn and soup. Add salt and pepper and blend well. Turn into a buttered casserole and bake in a 350° oven for 35 minutes. Garnish with pimiento and the remaining hot dog, cut into strips, set alternately over the top of the casserole.   *Serves 4.*

12 hot dogs
   6 *hard-boiled eggs*
   ¼ *cup salad dressing*
   1 *tablespoon vinegar*
   ½ *teaspoon dry mustard*
      Salt and pepper to taste
   3 *slices white toast, cut diagonally*
   ⅓ *cup condensed cream of celery soup*

**Hot Dog
and Egg
Casserole**

Peel the eggs and cut them in half lengthwise. Remove the yolks and beat until light and creamy with the salad dressing, vinegar, dry mustard and salt and pepper. Fill egg cavities with the mixture. Meanwhile, broil hot dogs for about 5 minutes, turning once. Using 6 individual casseroles, put a half-slice of toast into each with two stuffed eggs. Spoon the undiluted soup around and over the eggs. Place 2 hot dogs on top of each half-slice of toast. Bake in a 250° oven for 15 minutes.   *Serves 6.*

---

4 hot dogs
   1 *(10½ ounce) can condensed cream of celery soup*
   ¾ *cup milk*
   3 *teaspoons prepared mustard*
   1 *onion, minced*
   4 *potatoes, peeled, diced and cooked*

**Hot Dog–
Diced
Potato
Pie**

Combine the soup, milk, onion and mustard. Arrange this combination, the potatoes and the hot dogs, cut lengthwise, in layers in a buttered baking dish. Cover. Bake in a 400° oven for 30 minutes.
Serves 4.

Kidney Bean– Hot Dog– Curry Casserole

8 hot dogs
1 *clove garlic, minced*
2 *tablespoons butter or margarine, melted*
2 *onions, sliced thick*
4 *ribs celery, cut into ½-inch slices*
¼ *cup parsley, minced*
2 *pounds canned kidney beans*
¼ *teaspoon salt*
1 *tablespoon curry powder*

Sauté the hot dogs, cut into 1-inch slices, in the melted butter. When they are nearly browned, add the minced garlic and sauté a minute longer. Stir in the onions, celery and parsley. Sauté for 2 minutes. Add the kidney beans, salt and curry powder. Blend together. Turn into a casserole. Cover and bake 45 minutes in a 400° oven.   *Serves 6.*

Scalloped Potato– Hot Dog Casserole

6 hot dogs
3 *large onions, sliced very thin*
4½ *cups potatoes, sliced thin*
2 *teaspoons salt*
3 *tablespoons butter or margarine*
2 *tablespoons flour*
1 *teaspoon salt*
   Pepper to taste
¼ *teaspoon paprika*
2 *cups milk*
2 *tablespoons parsley, minced*
3 *thin slices Cheddar cheese*

Cook the onions and potatoes in one inch of boiling water to which 2 teaspoons salt have been added. After boiling 5 minutes, drain. Melt the butter in the top of a double boiler. Stir in the flour, 1 teaspoon salt, pepper, paprika and milk. Stirring constantly, cook until smooth and thick. In a 2-quart casserole, arrange one-third of the potato-onion mix-

ture topped with half the hot dogs, cut into halves
lengthwise, and minced parsley. Pour on one-third
of the sauce. Repeat in two more layers. Arrange the
slices of cheese on top, and bake for 35 minutes in
a 400° oven.   *Serves 4.*

---

8 hot dogs
  2 *onions, chopped*
  5 *tablespoons olive oil*
  1 *large eggplant*
    Flour
    Salt and pepper to taste
¼ *teaspoon thyme*
  1 *clove garlic, minced*
  1 *(1 pound) can Italian peeled tomatoes*

Hot Dog– Eggplant Casserole

Cook the onions in oil until transparent. Peel the
eggplant and cut it into chunks. Dust the chunks in
the flour. Add the eggplant chunks to the onions,
and sauté lightly. Add drained tomatoes. Blend in
the salt and pepper, thyme and garlic. Stirring frequently, cook until the eggplant is lightly browned.
Meanwhile, broil the hot dogs, split lengthwise,
until the cut surfaces are browned. Place the hot
dogs in the skillet with the eggplant mixture. Top
with hot mustard sauce.

  Hot mustard sauce:
  1 *egg*
  1 *tablespoon sugar*
¼ *teaspoon salt*
  3 *tablespoons dry mustard*
½ *cup vinegar*
  1 *tablespoon olive oil*

Beat the egg thoroughly. Stir in the sugar, salt, dry
mustard and vinegar. Cook over boiling water until as
thick as heavy cream. Remove from heat. Beat in the
olive oil.   *Serves 4 to 6.*

Hot Dog au Gratin Casserole

12 hot dogs
 4 *large tomatoes, sliced ¾-inch thick*
 1 *large onion, sliced very thin*
   Salt and pepper to taste
 1 *tablespoon butter or margarine*
 1 *cup Cheddar cheese, grated*

Arrange the tomato slices in a large, flame-proof casserole. Place onion slices on top of tomatoes. Sprinkle the salt and pepper over the onions. Arrange hot dogs on top. Dot with butter. Cover the casserole and cook 20 minutes, until the vegetables are tender. Sprinkle with the grated cheese. Cover and cook another 4 minutes. Serve in covered casserole.

Serves 6.

Hot Dog–Noodle Loaf

6 hot dogs
 1 *envelope dry smoky green pea soup mix*
 3 *cups hot water*
 1 *cup American cheese, shredded*
 ¼ *cup stuffed olives, sliced*
 1 *small onion, minced*
   Salt and pepper, to taste
 3 *cups uncooked broad egg noodles*

Cook the noodles until tender. Drain well. Add the hot water to the soup mix in a saucepan. Stir in the shredded cheese. Cook over moderate heat, stirring constantly until cheese is melted. Cut hot dogs into 1-inch slices. Add hot dog slices to soup mixture, along with sliced olives, minced onion and salt and pepper. Mix well. Pour half the noodles into a buttered, loaf-shaped baking dish. Top with half the soup mixture. Repeat the noodle and soup layers. Bake in a 350° oven for 20 minutes.   *Serves 4 to 6.*

8 hot dogs
   2 *cups cooked spinach, chopped and drained*
   2 *cups cooked rice*
   1 *can condensed cheese soup*
   2 *tablespoons milk*
  ½ *cup American cheese, grated*
   4 *teaspoons parsley, chopped*

Florentine Hot Dog Loaf

Preheat the oven to 375°. Arrange the spinach evenly over the bottom of a loaf-shaped, buttered baking dish. In a separate bowl, combine the rice, soup and milk. Spread this mixture evenly over the spinach. Arrange the hot dogs on top. Bake for 20 minutes. Then sprinkle the grated cheese over the hot dogs and bake for an additional 5 minutes, or until the cheese is melted. Remove from the oven. Sprinkle the chopped parsley over the hot dogs. Serve in the baking dish.   *Serves 4 to 5.*

---

12 hot dogs
  1⅓ *cups rice*
  1⅓ *cups water*
   ½ *teaspoon salt*
   2 *teaspoons prepared mustard*
   1 *can condensed cream of mushroom soup*
   ¼ *cup parsley, chopped*
   1 *small onion, minced*
   2 *tablespoons pimiento, chopped*
   ⅓ *cup Cheddar cheese, grated*

Hot Dogs Risotto

Combine the rice, water and salt in a saucepan and bring quickly to a boil. Remove from heat, fluff the rice with a fork. Cover quickly and allow to stand for 5 minutes. Combine rice with the soup, parsley, onion and pimiento. Slit the hot dogs lengthwise, but not completely through, to form "pockets." Stuff with the rice mixture. Sprinkle with grated cheese and bake in a 350° oven for 20 minutes.   *Serves 6.*

**Sweet-
n-Sour**

8 hot dogs
1 *large head cabbage, shredded*
¼ *cup butter or margarine, melted*
⅓ *cup vinegar*
¼ *cup brown sugar, packed*
2 *teaspoons caraway seed*
2 *teaspoons celery salt*
  Salt and pepper to taste

Stir the cabbage into the melted butter and cook
until lightly browned. Mix together all the remaining ingredients except the hot dogs. Stir this mixture into the cabbage. Place the hot dogs on top of
the cabbage mix. Cover tightly. Simmer for 8 minutes. Serve piping hot.   *Serves 4 to 8.*

Continental Dishes

12 hot dogs
  1 *cup pancake mix*
  ½ *cup corn meal*
1¾ *teaspoon chili powder*
  ¼ *teaspoon salt*
  2 *eggs, slightly beaten*
1½ *cups milk*
  2 *tablespoons shortening, melted*
  3 *cups Cheddar cheese, shredded*
  1 *cup chili sauce* ·
  1 *large onion, minced*

Hot Dog Enchiladas

Combine the pancake mix, corn meal, ¼ teaspoon chili powder and salt. Add the eggs, milk and melted shortening. Mix until smooth. Using about 3 tablespoons of batter for each pancake, cook 12 pancakes. Keep them warm in the oven while combining 2 cups of cheese, chili sauce, onion and remaining chili powder. Blend well. Spread on pancakes. Place a hot dog across each pancake, sprinkle with remaining cheese. Fold pancakes around hot dogs and serve. *Serves 6.*

39

Hot Dogs Amandine

8 hot dogs
    4 *ribs celery, diced*
    2 *tablespoons cooking oil*
    1 *(1 pound) can pineapple chunks*
    ¾ *cup water*
    1 *tablespoon soy sauce*
    1½ *tablespoons vinegar*
    2 *tablespoons cornstarch*
    1 *teaspoon ginger*
    ½ *teaspoon garlic salt*
    ½ *teaspoon monosodium glutamate*
    1 *green pepper, cut into 1 inch squares*
    ¼ *cup almonds, slivered*

Sauté the hot dogs, cut diagonally into thirds, and celery in the cooking oil. Drain pineapple chunks. Combine the pineapple juice with water, soy sauce and vinegar. Mix together the cornstarch, garlic salt and monosodium glutamate. Add pineapple juice mixture to the dry ingredients, and stir until free of lumps. Pour the pineapple juice combination over the hot dogs and celery. Stirring constantly, cook until thickened and clear. Add pineapple chunks and green pepper squares. Allow to simmer gently until pineapple chunks and pepper squares are hot. Sprinkle with almond slivers before serving

Serves 4.

Hot Dogs au Vin

8 hot dogs
    2 *tablespoons butter or margarine*
    3 *tablespoons chives, chopped*
    1 *garlic clove, minced*
    3 *cups burgundy wine*
    1 *(5 ounce) can pearl onions, drained*
    1 *(5 ounce) can button mushrooms*
    2 *cups brown gravy*
    1 *(10½ ounce) can tiny white potatoes, drained*

Sauté the hot dogs, cut crosswise into thirds, in the

butter. When the hot dogs are brown, remove from the skillet and set aside. Add the chives and garlic to the skillet and sauté. Slowly add the wine. Allow to simmer for 10 minutes. Add the onions, mushrooms and brown gravy. When it begins to simmer again, add the potatoes and browned hot dogs. Serve hot.

Serves 4.

Hot Dogs Orientale

6 hot dogs
 1 *large onion, sliced thin*
 1 *cup green pepper, slivered*
 4 *ribs celery, sliced diagonally*
 1 *tablespoon salad oil*
 1 *(11 ounce) can mandarin orange segments*
1½ *cups water*
 ¼ *cup white vinegar*
 ¼ *cup sugar*
 1 *beef bouillon cube*
 1 *teaspoon soy sauce*
 ½ *teaspoon salt*
 ½ *teaspoon monosodium glutamate*
 ¼ *teaspoon ginger*
 ⅛ *teaspoon fennel seed*
 ⅛ *teaspoon coarse black pepper*
 1 *tablespoon cornstarch*
3½ *cups sauerkraut, undrained*

Cook onion, green pepper and celery in oil over medium heat. Remove from skillet when tender and set aside. Lightly brown hot dogs, cut into ½-inch slices, in the same skillet. Drain syrup from oranges and reserve. Combine orange syrup with enough water to make 1¾ cups. Add this to the hot dogs. Stir in the vinegar, sugar, bouillon cube and seasonings. Bring to a boil. Blend cornstarch with ¼ cup cold water. Stir into boiling mixture and boil for one minute. Allow this to simmer while draining and washing the sauerkraut. Add sauerkraut and orange segments. Cover and heat. Serve with steamed rice.

Serves 4.

Hot Dogs Smetana

8 hot dogs
 1 *cup sour cream*
 ¼ *cup chives, chopped*
   Salt and pepper

Cut the hot dogs into ½-inch slices, then cut the slices into thin strips. Combine the other ingredients. Stir in the thin strips of hot dogs. Cover and refrigerate until ready to serve.   *Serves 4.*

Hot Dogs Alsatian

12 hot dogs
 ¼ *pound salt pork, cubed*
 2 *onions, sliced*
 1 *pound Italian sausage, halved crosswise*
 ½ *pound cooked ham, cubed*
 6 *cups sauerkraut, drained*
 3 *cups beef broth*
 ½ *teaspoon thyme*
   Salt and pepper to taste
 6 *peppercorns and 6 juniper berries, tied in cheesecloth bag*
10 *medium potatoes, pared and cooked*
 2 *tablespoons parsley, chopped*

Brown the salt pork in a large saucepan. Stir in the onions, sausage and ham. Cook until browned. Remove onion and meats from saucepan. Stir in sauerkraut; brown. Return onion and meats to saucepan. Stir in beef broth, salt and pepper and thyme; add cheesecloth bag with peppercorns and juniper berries. Cover. Simmer 45 minutes. Add the hot dogs, cut in half, and potatoes. Cover. Simmer 15 minutes. Remove cheesecloth bag. Arrange hot dogs and potatoes around the edge of a large platter. Pile sauerkraut mixture into the center. Sprinkle with parsley.
Serves 10.

16 hot dogs
  2 onions, *chopped*
  ¼ *cup butter or margarine*
  2 *vegetable bouillon cubes*
  1 *cup boiling water*
    Salt and pepper to taste
  1½ *teaspoons Worcestershire sauce*
  4 *cups sauerkraut, undrained*
  1½ *cups cooked rice*
  ⅔ *cup brown sugar, firmly packed*
  ¼ *cup parsley, chopped*
  2 *cups canned tomato sauce*
  ⅓ *cup dry sherry*
  ¼ *cup vinegar*
  ½ *cup canned Italian peeled tomatoes, drained*

**Hot Dogs
Madrid**

Brown the hot dogs, cut into 1-inch slices, and onion
in butter in a large skillet. Dissolve bouillon cubes
in the boiling water, and add to hot dogs. Add all
other ingredients and mix thoroughly. Cover and
cook over low heat for 20 minutes.   *Serves 8.*

---

12 hot dogs
  3 *tablespoons butter or margarine, melted*
  1 *small onion, minced*
  2 *tablespoons flour*
  2 *cups milk*
  ¼ *cup condensed tomato soup*
    Salt and pepper to taste
  1 *teaspoon sugar*

**Helsinki
Hot Dogs**

Sauté the onion in two tablespoons of butter until
it is tender, about three minutes. Stir in the flour and
cook until brown. Slowly add the milk, stirring constantly until the mixture thickens. Add condensed
tomato soup and salt, pepper and sugar. Blend well.
Sauté the hot dogs, cut into ½-inch slices, in the remaining tablespoon of butter until browned. Serve
topped with sauce.   *Serves 6.*

Hot Dogs
Oreganato

6 hot dogs
¼ *cup canned Italian tomatoes, drained*
2 *tablespoons sharp cheese, grated*
2 *tablespoons Parmesan cheese, grated*
1 *clove garlic, minced*
½ *teaspoon orégano, crushed*
   Pinch of sugar
6 *slices bacon*
6 *hot dog rolls, toasted*

Slit hot dogs lengthwise, but not completely through,
to form "pockets." Be careful not to cut to the
ends. Mix together tomatoes, two cheeses, garlic,
orégano and sugar and stuff the hot dogs. Wrap a
slice of bacon around each hot dog. Broil about 15
minutes over hot coals, or in the oven, turning frequently, until the filling is hot and the bacon crisp.
Place a hot dog in each toasted roll.   *Serves 3.*

Kabobs
Pizzaiola

8 hot dogs
1¼ *tablespoons salad oil*
1 *(1 pound) can pizza sauce*
16 *pieces green pepper, about 1 inch square*
16 *medium mushrooms*
8 *hot dog rolls, toasted*

Place hot dogs, cut into thirds, in a bowl. Combine
salad oil and pizza sauce to make Pizzaiola marinade.
Pour marinade over hot dogs and refrigerate for 2½
hours. Starting and ending with a piece of hot dog,
thread 3 hot dog pieces, 2 green pepper squares
and 2 mushrooms on a skewer. Place the 8 skewers
in a shallow pie plate or on a rack, about 4 inches
from heat. Broil 4 minutes on each side, basting
with marinade sauce during broiling. Serve in toasted
hot dog rolls.   *Serves 4.*

8 hot dogs
  1 *medium eggplant*
  ⅓ *cup flour*
     Salt and pepper to taste
  ¾ *cup olive oil*
  2 *cups tomato sauce*
  1 *cup Parmesan cheese, grated*
  1 *tablespoon orégano*
  4 *slices Mozzarella cheese*

Peel eggplant and cut into 8 ½-inch slices. Dredge slices in a mixture of flour, salt and pepper. Sauté floured eggplant slices in hot olive oil until golden brown, turning once. Place 4 eggplant slices side by side in a greased baking dish. Cut hot dogs into halves lengthwise. Top each slice with two hot dog halves. Spread with one cup of tomato sauce. Sprinkle with ½ cup of grated cheese and about half of the orégano. Repeat in another layer. Top with Mozzarella slices. Bake for 30 minutes in a 350° oven.   *Serves 4.*

Hot Dog Parmigiana

---

8 hot dogs
  3 *slices lean bacon, chopped*
  2 *small onions, chopped*
  6 *cups raw potatoes, diced*
  1 *cup water*
  2 *teaspoons paprika*
  1½ *teaspoons vinegar*
     Salt to taste

Fry the bacon in a heavy skillet. When the bacon is crisp, remove it and set aside. Add the onions to the bacon fat and cook slowly until tender. Add the potatoes and the water. Stir in the paprika, vinegar and salt. Allow to simmer for 5 minutes. Add the hot dogs, quartered, and bacon. Cover the pot and

simmer for 20 minutes.   *Serves 4.*

Potato Paprikash

**Spanish
Cabbage**

6 hot dogs
  6 cabbage leaves, parboiled
  6 teaspoons cheese, grated
  1 (8 ounce) package Spanish rice mix

Place a hot dog in the center of each slightly cooked cabbage leaf. Sprinkle each hot dog with a teaspoon of grated cheese. Fold the cabbage leaf over the hot dog. Meanwhile, prepare the Spanish rice according to the directions on the package. Turn it into a casserole, and top with cabbage rolls. Bake in a 350° oven for 15 minutes.   *Serves 6.*

**Coney
Island
Antipasto**

8 hot dogs
  1 head iceberg lettuce, separated
  3 tomatoes, cut into wedges
  8 slices Genoa salami
  4 pimientos, quartered
  8 ribs celery
  8 radishes
  8 stuffed green olives
  8 black olives
  8 anchovies

Arrange lettuce on a large platter. Cut hot dogs into ½-inch slices. Arrange all the other ingredients attractively on the platter. Serve with Garlic salad dressing.

Garlic Salad Dressing:
  ¼ cup olive oil
  ¼ cup wine vinegar
  2 garlic cloves, minced
  ¼ teaspoon basil, crushed
    Salt and pepper to taste

Combine the ingredients in a jar with a screw top 1 hour before using. Shake vigorously before pouring over antipasto.   *Serves 8.*

4 hot dogs
   1 *tablespoon butter or margarine, melted*
   1 *can condensed tomato soup*
   2 *tablespoons water*
   1 *teaspoon crushed orégano*
   1 *clove garlic, minced*
 ⅛ *teaspoon black pepper*
   1 *12-inch pizza shell*
   4 *slices Mozzarella cheese*
   1 *green pepper, cut into rings*
   1 *pimiento, cut into "diamonds"*

Hot Dog Pizza

Lightly brown the hot dogs, cut into thin slices, in the melted butter or margarine. Stir in the soup, water, orégano and garlic. Add the black pepper, and allow to simmer for 5 minutes, stirring occasionally. Pour this sauce on the pizza shell, spreading it to the edges. Arrange the cheese slices on top. Arrange pepper rings around edge of pizza. Place a pimiento "diamond" in the center of each pepper ring. Bake in a 400° oven for 20 minutes, until crust is crispy.
Serves 6.

---

8 hot dogs
   2 *tablespoons butter or margarine, melted*
   1 *small onion, minced*
   1 *rib of celery, minced*
   2 *tablespoons wine vinegar*
   1 *tablespoon prepared mustard*
 ¾ *cup strained borscht*
    Flour to thicken the borscht
   2 *tablespoons tomato catsup*

Borscht-Furters

Sauté the onion and celery in the melted butter or margarine. Slowly add the vinegar and prepared mustard. Then stir in the thickened borscht and tomato catsup. Add the hot dogs, and allow to simmer until hot.
Serves 4.

Hot Dog Lasagna

16 hot dogs
3 onions, sliced thin
½ cup olive oil
3 slices white bread, water-soaked and squeezed
2 eggs, unbeaten
¼ cup parsley, chopped
   Salt and pepper, to taste
2 cups cheese, grated
1 cup canned tomato sauce
2½ quarts canned Italian peeled tomatoes
2 pounds broad noodles
2½ pounds ricotta cheese
1 pound Mozzarella cheese, sliced

Sauté the onions in the oil and remove onions and set aside. Grind the hot dogs and combine with the bread, eggs, parsley, salt and pepper, and ½ cup grated cheese. Shape into small balls and sauté in the oil left in the skillet from the onions. Remove and set aside. Add tomato sauce and tomatoes to oil, cover and simmer for 1½ hours. Add meatballs and simmer another 1½ hours. Cook noodles according to package directions. Spoon enough sauce and meatballs into the bottom of a shallow roasting pan to cover the bottom. Top with crisscross layer of cooked noodles, then with half the ricotta cheese. Top with half the Mozzarella and one-third the remaining grated cheese. Repeat, ending with sauce topped with grated cheese. Make 7 deep gashes down through surface of noodles. Bake 40 minutes in a 350° oven.

Serves 10.

Salads

2 hot dogs
  ½ pound macaroni, uncooked
  1 (8 ounce) can spaghetti sauce
  8 ribs celery, sliced thin
  10 radishes, sliced thin
  ½ cup sweet pickle, diced
  2 hard-boiled eggs, chopped
  ¾ cup mayonnaise
  ¼ cup evaporated milk
  1 tablespoon pickle juice
  2 tablespoons prepared mustard
  1 tablespoon instant minced onion
    Salt and pepper to taste
  2 tomatoes, cut into quarters
    Paprika

West-
chester
Hot Dog
Salad

Cook the macaroni according to the package directions. Drain, rinse with cold water and drain again. Sprinkle with the spaghetti sauce. Add all the other ingredients except the tomatoes, hot dogs and paprika. Place in a large bowl and chill.

Arrange tomato wedges around edges of bowl. Sprinkle hot dogs, cut into ½-inch slices, on top of all. Sprinkle paprika on top of hot dogs. *Serves 8.*

**Hot Dog
and Bean
Salad**

8 hot dogs
 1 (1 *pound*) *can red kidney beans, drained*
 1 (1 *pound*) *can white kidney beans, drained*
 1 (1 *pound*) *can chick peas, drained*
 ⅓ *cup vinegar*
 4 *scallions, chopped*
 ¼ *cup olive oil*
 ¼ *cup green pepper, chopped*
 4 *ribs celery, minced*
   Salt and pepper to taste
 1 *tomato, cut into wedges*

Cut hot dogs into ½-inch slices. Combine all the ingredients, except the tomato wedges, and chill. Turn into a large bowl, garnish with tomato wedges and serve.   *Serves 8.*

**Hot Dog
and
Potato
Salad**

6 hot dogs
 4 *slices bacon*
 1 (5½ *ounce*) *package scalloped potato mix*
 2¾ *cups water*
 3 *tablespoons vinegar*
 1 *onion, finely chopped*
 2 *teaspoons prepared mustard*

In a large skillet, fry the bacon until crisp. Drain on paper towels. Brown the hot dogs, quartered, in bacon fat. Drain on paper towels, then drain the fat from the skillet. Turn the scalloped potato mix (potatoes and seasoning) into the skillet. Stir in the water. Bring to a boil. Cover, and allow to simmer for 25 minutes, until the potatoes are tender. Stir in the vinegar, onion and mustard. Add the hot dogs, and heat through. Serve garnished with crumbled bacon.   *Serves 4 to 6.*

5 hot dogs
  2 *cups cabbage, shredded*
  8 *ribs celery, minced*
  1 *tablespoon sugar*
  Salt and white pepper to taste
  1 *teaspoon onion, minced*
  1 *tablespoon vinegar*
  ⅓ *cup light cream*
  1 *tablespoon prepared mustard*
  ¼ *cup cooked salad dressing*

Hot Dog Slaw

Chop the hot dogs very fine. Combine all the ingredients in a salad bowl, tossing thoroughly. Chill and serve. *Serves 4.*

---

6 hot dogs
  6 *cooked potatoes, sliced*
  6 *slices bacon*
  1½ *tablespoons flour*
  1 *cup water*
  ⅓ *cup vinegar*
  Salt and pepper to taste
  1 *tablespoon sugar*
  2 *ribs celery, sliced thin*
  ½ *small head romaine lettuce*
  6 *radishes, sliced thin*
  2 *onions, sliced thin*

Hot Dog Romaine Salad

Cook the bacon until crisp. Slice hot dogs diagonally into 8 pieces each. Brown the slices in bacon fat; remove from skillet. Set aside with potatoes and bacon. Add flour and water to the bacon fat in the skillet, stirring until smooth. Add vinegar, salt and pepper, and sugar. Stirring constantly, cook over a low fire until thickened. Add a layer of sliced potatoes, a layer of hot dogs and one each of celery, romaine, radishes and onions. Repeat until all are used. Toss very gently. Top with crumbled bacon. *Serves 6.*

**Easy
Hot Dog
Salad
Bowl**

8 hot dogs
1 (*1 pound*) *can red kidney beans, drained*
½ *cup sour pickles, sliced*
1 *cup French dressing*
1 *onion, sliced very thin*
1 *head lettuce, torn into bite-size bits*

Combine beans, hot dogs, cut into ½-inch slices, pickles and half of the dressing. Chill thoroughly. In a salad bowl, alternate layers of torn lettuce, bean mixture and onion slices. Pour remaining dressing over all and chill. *Serves 6.*

**Garden
Green
Salad**

8 hot dogs
½ *pound uncooked elbow macaroni*
4 *ribs celery, sliced on an angle*
1 *large cucumber, pared and diced*
⅓ *cup green peppers, minced*
1 *small onion, minced*
8 *stuffed olives, sliced*
¼ *cup liquid drained from olives*
4 *hard-boiled eggs, chopped*
1 *cup cooked salad dressing*
2 *teaspoons prepared mustard*
Salt and pepper to taste

Cook macaroni according to package directions. Drain, rinse thoroughly with cold water, and drain again. Chill. Combine the chilled, cooked macaroni with the other ingredients and the hot dogs, sliced thin diagonally. Mix together and chill before serving. *Serves 8.*

8 hot dogs
  ½ *pound macaroni, cooked*
  1 *quart cabbage, finely shredded*
  2 *green peppers, finely chopped*
  2 *scallions, sliced very thin*
  1 *tablespoon prepared horseradish*
  2 *teaspoons vinegar*
  1 *cup dairy sour cream*
     Salt and pepper to taste

**Macaroni–
Hot Dog
Cabbage
Salad**

Combine all the ingredients, except the hot dogs.
Mix thoroughly, and chill. Arrange in a mound in a
low bowl. Surround with hot dogs cut into halves
crosswise and serve.   *Serves 4 to 6.*

---

8 hot dogs
  1 *(1 pound) head cabbage*
  2 *tablespoons butter or margarine, melted*
     Salt and pepper to taste
  1½ *tablespoons lemon juice*

**Hot
Hot Dog
Slaw**

Shred the cabbage and cook it for 5 minutes in one
inch of boiling water in a covered pot. Drain, reserving ½ cup of cabbage water. Sprinkle the melted
butter over the cabbage. Add cabbage water, salt,
pepper and lemon juice. Arrange hot dogs, cut into
½-inch slices, over all. Cover the pot and allow to
simmer for 8 minutes. Meanwhile, heat a shallow
vegetable dish. Place the hot slaw in the dish and
serve.   *Serves 8.*

Hot Dog Salad Dressing

8 hot dogs
½ teaspoon dry mustard
2 tablespoons milk
1 tablespoon pickle relish
⅓ cup salad dressing

Grind the hot dogs coarsely. Mix together all the ingredients. Chill and serve over bean or potato or lettuce salad.   *Serves 6.*

Party Dishes and Appetizers

8 hot dogs
1 (10½ ounce) can condensed cream of mush-
    room soup
1 (3 ounce) can sliced mushrooms, drained
½ cup milk
4 slices American cheese, shredded
½ teaspoon prepared mustard
  Paprika
4 slices Italian bread, toasted

Hot Dog– Mushroom Rarebit

Blend soup and milk in the top of a double boiler, over a low flame. Add cheese and mustard and place the pan over hot water. Stir and heat until cheese melts. Add the hot dogs, cut into ½-inch slices, and heat thoroughly. Pour over toast. Sprinkle with paprika. For buffet suppers, the rarebit may be kept warm in a covered chafing dish. *Serves 4.*

Hot Dogs au Vin Blanc

8 hot dogs
   ¾ *cup butter or margarine*
   ½ *cup dry white wine*

Sauté the hot dogs, diagonally cut into 5 slices, in ¼ cup of melted butter until very lightly browned. Set aside. Melt the remaining butter in a casserole with a fitted cover. Stir in the wine. Add the hot dog slices, cover and heat in a 250° oven until hot through, about 45 minutes. Serve speared with toothpicks and with a sauce or mustard for dipping.
Serves 10 or makes 40 appetizers.

Hot Dog Corn Dots

3 hot dogs
   3 *egg yolks*
   1⅔ *cups frozen whole-kernel corn*
      Salt and pepper to taste
   ¼ *cup sifted flour*
   3 *egg whites, beaten stiff*
      Shortening for deep frying

Beat the egg yolks until light. Add the corn and hot dogs, grated. Mix in the salt, pepper and flour. Fold in the stiffly beaten egg whites. Heat the shortening to 370°. Drop the batter by spoonfuls into the hot fat. Turning once, fry a few at a time until a delicate golden brown. Drain on paper towels.
Serves 6 or makes 12 canapés.

Hot Dogs à Go Go

24 hot dogs
   1 *pound Cheddar cheese, grated*
   1 *cup pickle relish*
   1 *cup mayonnaise*
   ½ *cup chili sauce*
   ¼ *cup prepared mustard*
   24 *hot dog rolls*

Mix together cheese, pickle relish, chili sauce and mustard. Slit hot dogs lengthwise to form "pockets." Spread cheese mixture in the pockets. Place a hot dog in each roll. Wrap the roll in aluminum foil. Just before the party begins, put the wrapped hot dogs in a hot oven or on the grill. Bake until hot and serve.   *Serves 12.*

Hot Dog Treats

4 hot dogs
   4 slices white bread, crusts trimmed
   2 teaspoons cheese spread
   2 teaspoons butter or margarine, melted

Place a hot dog across a slice of bread. Spread ½ teaspoon cheese along the hot dog. Wrap bread around it. Cut the wrapped hot dog into four pieces, securing each tiny rollup with a toothpick. Place in a shallow baking dish. Brush with melted butter. Bake for 10 minutes in a 325° oven.
                        Serves 4 or makes 16 appetizers.

Hot Dog Bites

4 hot dogs
   4 chunks pineapple
   4 cooked apricots, pitted
   4 cooked prunes, pitted
   8 slices bacon

Cut hot dogs in quarters. String 4 chunks of hot dogs and 4 chunks of pineapple on 4 separate picks. Wrap in ½ slice of bacon. Stuff the apricots and prunes with a chunk of hot dog and wrap in bacon. Wrap 4 plain chunks of hot dog in bacon. Secure bacon on all canapés with toothpicks. Broil all until browned.   *Serves 4 or makes 16 appetizers.*

Hot Dog Wheel

12 hot dogs
  2 *hard-boiled eggs, chopped fine*
  1 *rib celery, diced*
  ¼ *cup stuffed Spanish olives, chopped*
  ⅔ *cup mayonnaise*
  2 *teaspoons prepared mustard*
    Salt and pepper to taste
  6 *large lettuce leaves*
  1 *tomato, sliced thin*
  ½ *Bermuda onion, sliced thin*
  8 *radishes*
  8 *black olives*

Finely chop 6 hot dogs. Cut the 6 remaining hot dogs in halves, lengthwise and then across. Combine the chopped hot dogs, eggs, celery, stuffed olives, mayonnaise, mustard and salt and pepper. Arrange lettuce leaves on a large round platter. Arrange the hot dog mixture in a mound on top of the lettuce bed. Arrange the hot dog quarters spoke fashion on top of the mixture. With alternate slices of tomato and onion along the edge of the platter, make a "tire" for the wheel. Garnish with radishes and olives.   *Serves 12.*

Hot Dog Olive Boats

8 hot dogs
  8 *slices bread*
    Mustard
    Melted butter
  24 *stuffed Spanish olives*

Spread bread with mustard. Place a hot dog diagonally on each side. Bring bread corners to the top of the hot dog, and fasten with toothpicks. Brush with melted butter, and brown in hot oven. Spear an olive on each toothpick end.   *Serves 4.*

6 hot dogs
   Oil for deep frying
   1 *cup flour, sifted*
   ¼ *teaspoon salt*
   1 *egg, beaten*
   ¾ *cup milk*
   1 *teaspoon salad oil*
   1 *garlic clove, minced*
   4 *teaspoons onion, grated*

**Hot Dog
and Onion
Fritters**

Heat oil to 370°. Mix togther flour and salt. Mix together in a separate bowl the egg, milk, salad oil, garlic and onion. Add this mixture to the flour mixture. Blend until smooth. Dip the hot dogs, cut into ½-inch slices, into the batter, coating them well. Drop them, one at a time, into the hot oil. When they float and are browned underneath, turn them with a fork to brown the other sides. Drain on absorbent paper.   *Serves 8 or makes 42 appetizers.*

---

8 hot dogs
   1 *package pastry mix*
   4 *wedges Roquefort cheese*

**Hot Dog
Turnovers**

Prepare the pastry mix as directed on the package, rolling it out to a thickness of ⅛ inch. Cut into rectangles 1 inch longer than the hot dogs and wide enough to wrap around them, with an additional ½ inch for overlapping. Cut each wedge of cheese into halves. Crumble one half on a line down the center of the rectangle of pastry. Place a hot dog on each line of cheese. Dampen the edge of the pastry and wrap the pastry around the frank, sealing the edges and the ends. Bake in a 500° oven until golden brown.   *Serves 8.*

Hot Dog Snacks

8 hot dogs
2 *tablespoons butter or margarine, melted*
1 *teaspoon coarse black pepper*
1 *teaspoon marjoram*

Sauté hot dogs, sliced into 5 pieces diagonally, in the melted butter, adding pepper and marjoram. Turn constantly. When nicely browned, turn into a warm chafing dish. Spear with toothpicks.

Serves 8 or makes 40 appetizers.

Hot Dog Tidbits

8 *hot dogs*
8 *stuffed green olives*
8 *cubes Cheddar cheese*
8 *pickled onions*
8 *chunks dill pickle*

Quarter hot dogs. Using 32 toothpicks, string a chunk of hot dog between 2 olives, 2 cubes of cheese, 2 onions and 2 chunks of pickle until all ingredients are used. Arrange the kebobs on a canapé tray.

Serves 6 or makes 32 appetizers.

Hot Dog Canapés

8 hot dogs
½ *cup mayonnaise*
a mixture of grated cheese and prepared mustard
a mixture of chopped olives and curry powder
a mixture of chopped dates and grated orange rind
a mixture of chunky peanut butter and minced celery
a mixture of cheese spread and tomato catsup
Melba toast and toasted bread cut into squares and rectangles

Chop the hot dogs and combine with the mayonnaise. Divide the hot dogs into five bowls; combine with the other mixtures, made up to your taste, making five different spreads. Spread the five mixtures on Melba toast and toasted bread for a cocktail assortment.   *Serves 8 or makes 40 canapés.*

---

3 hot dogs
   ¼ *cup cheese, grated*
   1 *hard-boiled egg, chopped*
   4 *hamburger rolls*

Hot Dog
Stuffed
Roll
Appetizers

Mince the hot dogs and mix together with the cheese and egg. Scoop out the rolls and stuff with the hot dog mixture. Wrap in foil and place in refrigerator until ready to use. Bake for 10 minutes in a 350° oven. Cut into bite-size portions.
Serves 6 or makes 24 appetizers.

---

4 hot dogs
   2 *tablespoons salad oil*
   ½ *cup chili sauce*
   3 *tablespoons prepared mustard*
   1 *tablespoon horseradish*

Puffed
Hot Dogs

Cut hot dogs into thin, round slices. Sauté in salad oil until browned and puffed on both sides. Combine chili sauce, mustard and horseradish and serve as a dunking sauce for the hot dogs. Without the sauce, hot dogs cooked this way are excellent with scrambled eggs.   *Serves 4 as appetizers.*

Hot Dog Nibble Tray

4 hot dogs
½ *pound loaf cheese, cut into ¼-inch cubes*
1 *can cubed fruit*
1 *jar maraschino cherries*

Cut hot dogs into ¼-inch slices and arrange on cocktail picks with cheese and canned fruit cubes, alternating hot dog chunks, cheese and fruit. Chill for 30 minutes, and serve. *Makes 16.*

Double Dip

6 hot dogs
1 *small onion, minced*
1 *rib of celery, sliced thin*
¼ *cup sweet pickle juice*
4 *drops of liquid hot pepper seasoning*
3 *ounces cream cheese*
2 *tablespoons pineapple juice concentrate, thawed*
Thick potato chips, for dipping

Chop 4 hot dogs fine and grind together with onion and celery. Stir in the pickle juice and hot pepper seasoning. Place in a dipping bowl. Mince the remaining hot dogs and mix together with all the remaining ingredients except the potato chips. Place in a separate dipping bowl. Place the two bowls on a large tray. Heap the thick potato chips around the bowls on the tray.

Barbecues and Picnics

24 hot dogs
 2 *large onions, chopped fine*
 1¼ *cups tomato catsup*
 ½ *cup water*
 ¼ *cup salad oil*
 2 *tablespoons Worcestershire sauce*
 1½ *tablespoons vinegar*
 2 *teaspoons liquid smoke*
  Salt and pepper to taste
 ½ *teaspoon dry mustard*

Combine all the ingredients except the hot dogs in a saucepan. Simmer about 15 minutes uncovered. Meanwhile, string the hot dogs—just like beads—on a cord, allowing 6 hot dogs for each string. Use a skewer with an eye for the needle, and be sure to knot cord each time you thread a hot dog. Now, one at a time, loop the 4 hot dog strings over the rod of a wire clothes hanger. Knot together the two cord ends of each hot dog string to form 4 full loops. Slash the hot dogs on both sides. Leaving hanger to dangle over the sides of the outdoor grill, place the hot dogs over the hot coals and grill until done on one side. To turn, pick up hanger handle and turn all the hot dogs at once; grill for a few more minutes. Dunk the hot dogs into saucepan. Carry the dunked hot dogs to each person—along with scissors to snip them off the string. Pass the remaining sauce.

Serves 10 to 12.

69

Hot Dog Nutty Fritters

8 hot dogs
  8 *tablespoons peanut butter*
  8 *strips bacon*
  8 *hot dog rolls, toasted*

Slit the hot dogs lengthwise, but not completely through, to form "pockets." Fill each pocket with a level tablespoon of peanut butter. Wrap each hot dog with a spiral of bacon, securing the bacon on each end with a toothpick. Starting with the split side down, grill over hot coals until the bacon is crisp. Serve in hot dog rolls.   *Serves 4.*

Hawaiian Hot Dog Kabobs

4 hot dogs
  1 (*10½ ounce*) *can pineapple chunks*
  4 *teaspoons vegetable oil*
  8 *hot dog rolls, toasted*
  8 *teaspoons barbecue sauce*

Alternate each hot dog, cut into 5 chunks, on a skewer with pineapple chunks. Brush with vegetable oil. Broil over hot coals, turning until browned. Meanwhile, spread each roll with barbecue sauce. Slide hot dogs off skewers and onto the rolls.
          Serves 4.

Stuffed Hot Dog Barbecue

8 hot dogs
  4 *teaspoons mustard*
  4 *teaspoons catsup*
  1 (*1 pound*) *can sauerkraut*

Split hot dogs lengthwise to form a "pocket." Spread the cut surfaces of 4 hot dogs with mustard and the other 4 with catsup. Place 3 to 4 tablespoons of drained sauerkraut on each mustard hot dog. Top

with a hot dog coated with catsup. Secure ends with
toothpick. Wrap each hot dog "sandwich" in a
double thickness of heavy-duty aluminum foil. Place
on briquets or coals and grill about 4 minutes on
each side.   *Serves 4.*

**Hot Dog
Party
Puffs**

12 hot dogs
  2 *cups biscuit mix*
  ⅔ *cup milk*
  ½ *cup cheese, grated*
 12 *strips bacon*

Add the milk to the biscuit mix. Using a fork, stir
into a soft dough. Beat this dough until it is stiff and
sticky, about 1½ dozen strokes. Stir in the grated
cheese. Pat the dough around the hot dogs to make
a thin covering. Wrap a strip of bacon around each
dough-encased hot dog, securing the ends with toothpicks. Roast over coals or fire. Serve in paper napkins.
Serves 6.

**Boston
Barbecue**

8 hot dogs
  4 *teaspoons mustard*
  1 *cup canned baked beans*

Slit the hot dogs lengthwise to form a "pocket."
Spread cut surfaces with mustard. Fill pockets with
drained beans, and secure with toothpicks. Barbecue
in a hand grill over medium heat, turning several
times, until the beans are hot.   *Serves 4.*

**Polynesian
Barbecue**

8 hot dogs
1 (10½ ounce) *can crushed pineapple*
8 *slices bacon*

Slit the hot dogs lengthwise to form a "pocket."
Fill pockets with drained pineapple. Wrap a slice
of bacon around each stuffed hot dog, securing ends
with toothpicks. Barbecue in hand grill over medium
heat, turning several times, until the bacon is crisp.
Serves 4.

**Texas
Chili
Hot Dogs**

8 hot dogs
1 *can (15 ounces) chili with beans*
8 *hot dog rolls, toasted*
⅓ *cup Bermuda onions, chopped*
½ *cup Longhorn cheese, grated*
2 *green chile peppers, minced*

Slash hot dogs and grill over coals. Heat the chili.
Place a hot dog on a roll and lavishly spoon chili
over it. Sprinkle with onions, cheese (Cheddar may
be substituted) and green chiles.   *Serves 4.*

**Astronauts'
Delight**

8 hot dogs
3 *dill pickles*
1 *onion, chopped*
¼ *cup butter or margarine, melted*
1 *cup canned tomato sauce*
1 *cup water*
2 *tablespoons sugar*
¼ *teaspoon sage*
½ *teaspoon dry mustard*
  Dash black pepper
1 *tablespoon vinegar*

1 *tablespoon Worcestershire sauce*
1 *head cabbage*

Cut hot dogs into 2 pieces and pickles into 1-inch chunks. Thread a piece of hot dog lengthwise on a skewer, then a pickle chunk, then another chunk of hot dog. Broil over hot coals. Mix together all the other ingredients, except the head of cabbage. Brush the skewers with this sauce as they cook. To serve, stick skewers into cabbage head. Pass remaining sauce. *Serves 4.*

Minted Kabobs

8 hot dogs
1 (*10½ ounce*) *can pineapple chunks*
½ *cup soy sauce*
¼ *cup honey*
2 *tablespoons salad oil*
1 *teaspoon dry mustard*
⅓ *cup wine vinegar*
2 *tablespoons fresh mint, finely chopped*
½ *cup catsup*
16 *small white onions, parboiled*
½ *pound large mushrooms*
2 *tomatoes, cut into wedges*

Drain off ¼ cup of syrup from pineapple and combine with soy sauce, honey, oil, mustard, vinegar, mint and catsup. Blend thoroughly by beating. Pour this marinade over the hot dogs, cut into ½-inch slices. Refrigerate for one hour. Thread the marinated hot dogs, pineapple chunks, onions, mushrooms, and tomato wedges on skewers. Brush with the marinade and cook over coals until hot dog slices are glazed, continuing to brush with marinade while turning the skewer. *Serves 4.*

**Surprise
Packages**

8 hot dogs
¼ *cup cheese, grated*
1½ *teaspoons prepared mustard*
2 *hard-cooked eggs, chopped*
1 *teaspoon steak sauce*
2 *tablespoons pickle relish, drained*
¼ *teaspoon garlic salt*
¼ *cup chili sauce*
8 *hot dog rolls*

Mince the hot dogs, then mix together with all the ingredients except the rolls. Hollow out centers of rolls. Fill with hot dog mixture and close. Wrap each stuffed roll in heavy-duty aluminum foil. Refrigerate until a half-hour before using. When ready to use, put wrapped rolls on grill, close to coals. Turning often, grill for about 20 minutes, until the filling is heated.   *Serves 4.*

**Stuffed
Zucchini**

4 hot dogs
4 *small zucchini squash*
½ *cup highly seasoned catsup*
Dash hot pepper sauce
1 *teaspoon seasoned salt*
1 *teaspoon orégano, crushed*
Dash black pepper
Butter or margarine
¼ *cup Parmesan cheese, grated*

Cutting only three fourths of the way through to the bottom, slice each zucchini twice lengthwise. Mix catsup and seasonings, and spoon a little of the mixture into both slits. Cut each hot dog in half lengthwise. Wedge hot dog halves, cut side down, into zucchini slits. Place each zucchini on a piece of aluminum foil. Dot with butter and sprinkle with grated cheese. Fold the foil over the zucchini, leaving space for steam to escape, and heat over coals until tender—about 1 hour.   *Serves 4.*

8 hot dogs **Smokeys**
  Liquid smoke
  1 *cup sauerkraut*
  ¼ *cup chili sauce*
  ¾ *teaspoon caraway seed*
  8 *strips bacon*
  8 *hot dog rolls*

Slit hot dogs lengthwise to form a "pocket." Brush cut surfaces with liquid smoke. Mix together the drained sauerkraut, chili sauce and caraway seed. Stuff the hot dogs with this mixture. Wrap each hot dog with a strip of bacon, securing each end with a toothpick. Place over hot coals, turning until bacon is crisp—about 15 minutes. *Serves 4.*

---

8 hot dogs **Hot Dog**
  ½ *pound American cheese, shredded* **Loaf**
  1 *small onion, minced*
  ¼ *cup green pepper, minced*
  ¼ *cup chili sauce*
  1 *tablespoon prepared mustard*
  1 *clove garlic*
  ¼ *cup butter or margarine*
  1 *large loaf Italian bread*

Combine cheese, onion, green pepper, chili sauce and mustard. Mix thoroughly. Crush garlic and cream it together with the butter, then remove garlic. Cut the Italian bread into slices about ½ inch thick, cutting every other slice not quite through to the bottom crust. Spread inside surfaces of each sandwich with the garlic butter and the cheese mixture. Now, fashioning them in the pattern of a spoke, arrange hot dogs, cut into quarters, in each sandwich. Line up the sandwiches in the shape of the original loaf of bread on a double thickness of aluminum foil. Wrap securely. On the cool section of the charcoal grill heat the wrapped loaf about 25 minutes, until the cheese melts. *Serves 4.*

**Cottage
Barbecue**

8 hot dogs
1 *cup cottage cheese with chives*
8 *hot dog rolls*
8 *strips bacon*
1 *cup bottled barbecue sauce*

Slit the hot dogs lengthwise to form a "pocket."
Stuff with the cottage cheese. Spiral wrap a strip of
bacon around each hot dog, securing the ends with
toothpicks. Broil in a foil pan over hot coals, until
bacon is crisp. When almost done, add the barbecue
sauce.   *Serves 4.*

**Hot Dogs
on a Raft**

8 hot dogs
8 *slices bacon*
8 *strips pickle*
8 *strips cheese*
8 *hot dog rolls, toasted and buttered*

Slit hot dogs lengthwise to form a "pocket." Grill
over hot coals. Place bacon on a sheet of heavy-duty
aluminum foil, turning up the edges of the foil to
catch bacon drippings. Place on top of grill and
cook until bacon is crisp. Drain off bacon fat and
reserve bacon. Insert a strip of pickle and cheese in
each hot dog pocket. Place on the foil and heat until
the cheese melts. Place two stuffed hot dogs crosswise
on two hot dog rolls to form a "raft." Lay two slices
of bacon across the hot dogs to tie the raft together.
                                          Serves 4.

**Hot Dog
Bag of
Beans**

4 hot dogs
Liquid smoke
2 *cups pork and beans in molasses sauce*
1 *(6 ounce) roll sharp cheese, sliced*

Take a 3 foot length of 18-inch wide aluminum foil; fold it in half to make an 18- by 18-inch square. Arrange hot dogs in a square, ends to ends, in the center part of the foil square. Brush hot dogs lightly with liquid smoke. Spoon the beans into the center of the hot dog square. Bring up the corners of the foil. Twist the top as a paper bag. Heat over low coals about 35 minutes, until hot. Open the foil, crumpling down the sides to make a serving dish. Circle the cheese slices over the hot dogs. Leave on heat until cheese melts. *Serves 4.*

---

2 hot dogs
   1 *cup corned beef, shredded*
   ¾ *cup American cheese, shredded*
   ½ *cup stuffed Spanish olives, chopped*
   ¼ *cup tomato catsup*
   2 *teaspoons Worcestershire sauce*
   4 *tablespoons green onion, finely chopped*
1½ *teaspoons green pepper, finely chopped*
   8 *hot dog rolls*

Corned Beef Coneys

Chop the hot dogs and combine with corned beef, olives, catsup, Worcestershire sauce, onion and green pepper. Fill the rolls with this mixture, and wrap each roll in aluminum foil. Place on hot coals and cook until cheese is melted, about 20 minutes. *Serves 8.*

**Pickle
Kabobs**

8 hot dogs
   2 *onions, quartered*
   8 *small sweet pickles*
   ⅓ *cup chili sauce*
   1 *tablespoon vinegar*
1½ *teaspoon granulated brown sugar*

Cut each hot dog into three pieces. On each skewer, thread alternately a piece of hot dog, an onion quarter and a pickle. Mix together the chili sauce, vinegar and brown sugar. Brush this sauce over the kabobs. Cook the kabobs three inches from heat for about 3 minutes on each side. Serve on oblong plates.   *Serves 8.*

Hot Dogs for Children

8 hot dogs
    4 *slices American cheese*
    1 *can crescent refrigerator rolls*

**Cheese
Hot Dog
Roll-Ups**

Preheat the oven to 375°. Parboil hot dogs. Split them lengthwise, almost through. Slice cheese into strips. Insert strips of cheese into each hot dog slit. Separate the crescent rolls into triangles. Wrap each hot dog in a roll. Bake the roll-ups for about 10 minutes or until the rolls turn golden brown.

Serves 4 to 8.

---

8 hot dogs
    Butter or margarine
    8 *hamburger rolls, toasted*
    2 *teaspoons mustard*

**Round
Hot Dogs**

Slash hot dogs crosswise, almost through at ½ inch intervals. Sauté the hot dogs in butter. Turn them as they brown and curl into doughnut shape. Place a hot dog on each roll and spread with mustard.

Serves 4 to 8.

81

**Corney
Hot Dogs**

8 hot dogs
½ *cup tomato catsup*
½ *cup corn flake crumbs*

Spiralling from end to end, score hot dogs lightly.
Insert a wooden popsickle skewer in the end of
each hot dog. Roll each hot dog in tomato catsup and
then in the crumbs until generously coated. Place
the hot dogs in a shallow foil-lined baking dish leaving spaces between them. Bake for 15 minutes in a
350° oven.   *Serves 4 to 8.*

**Golden
Stuffed
Hot Dogs**

8 hot dogs
1 *tablespoon flour*
1 *egg, well-beaten*
  Salt and pepper to taste
2 *cups mashed potatoes, cold*
¼ *cup Cheddar cheese, grated*
¼ *cup onion, minced*

Place hot dogs in a covered saucepan of boiling
water; turn off the heat and allow the hot dogs to
stand in the hot water for 15 minutes. Blend together the other ingredients in the order listed. Split
each hot dog lengthwise, but not completely through,
to form a "pocket." Stuff with potato mixture. Bake
in a 450° oven until the potatoes are golden brown,
about 10 minutes.   *Serves 4 to 8.*

**Hot Dog
Sloppy
Joes**

8 hot dogs
1 *pound ground beef*
2 *tablespoons vegetable oil*
1 *cup canned tomato sauce*
1 *onion, minced*
2 *tablespoons water*
8 *hot dog rolls*

Brown the beef in vegetable oil in a heavy skillet.
Split the hot dogs lengthwise, and add them to the
beef. Add tomato sauce, onion and water. Allow to
simmer for 15 minutes. Meanwhile heat the buns
in the oven. Place two hot dog halves on each
roll. Spoon chopped mixture generously over each
heated roll.   *Serves 4 to 8.*

Hot Dog Pizzas

8 hot dogs
   8 *hot dog rolls*
     Butter or margarine
   ¼ *pound Mozzarella cheese*
   ½ *cup canned tomato sauce*
     Parmesan cheese, grated

Split the rolls and spread with butter. Toast lightly
under broiler. Place a strip of Mozzarella cheese on
each roll. Split hot dogs lengthwise and place half a
hot dog on each roll half. Top each with a tablespoon of tomato sauce and a short strip of Mozzarella
cheese. Sprinkle with grated Parmesan cheese. Broil
until cheese melts.   *Serves 4 to 8.*

Peanut Butter Hot Dogs

8 hot dogs
   8 *tablespoons peanut butter*
   8 *hot dog rolls, toasted*

Boil hot dogs in a cup of water for 5 minutes. Cover
and allow to stand 5 minutes. Meanwhile, spread
peanut butter on cut surfaces of hot dog rolls. Place
a hot dog on each peanut-buttered roll.
                                   Serves 4 to 8.

Cheese Hot Dogs

8 hot dogs
8 *hot dog rolls*
8 *slices American cheese*

Slice each hot dog into thirds, lengthwise, and flatten it along one sliced roll. Place a slice of cheese on top of each hot dog. Broil until cheese melts.

Serves 4 to 8.

Freezer Hot Dogs

24 hot dogs
24 *strips American cheese*
24 *strips bacon*
24 *hot dog rolls, toasted*

Split hot dogs and insert a strip of cheese into each "pocket." Wrap each hot dog with a strip of bacon, securing the ends with toothpicks. Wrap a pair of stuffed hot dogs in a piece of aluminum foil, forming 12 sets of freezer packs. Stack the packs in the freezer until ready to use. When ready to cook, open one side of each pack. Broil in the improvised pan for 8 minutes, turning once, until bacon is crisp. Serve on hot dog rolls. *Serves 12 to 24.*

Fritter Pops

40 hot dogs
2 *cups flour, sifted*
1 *tablespoon baking powder*
1 *teaspoon salt*
4 *tablespoons sugar*
4 *eggs, well-beaten*
2 *cups milk*
3 *tablespoons salad oil*
Flour

Sift the flour, baking powder, salt and sugar in a large mixing bowl. In a separate bowl mix together the eggs, milk and oil. Stir the wet ingredients into the dry ingredients in the large bowl. Roll the hot dogs in flour, shaking off excess flour. Dip floured hot dogs into the large bowl of batter, coating each hot dog thoroughly. Fry in deep fat at 375° for 4 to 6 minutes. Drain. Spear each hot dog with a wooden skewer to make a fritter pop.   *Serves 20 to 40.*

---

8 hot dogs
  8 *slices bacon*
  8 *slices raisin bread*
  ⅓ *cup pickle relish*
  2 *tablespoons prepared mustard*

Raisin Bread Hot Dogs

Grill the bacon slightly and set aside. Place hot dogs in boiling water, cover, remove from heat and allow to stand 5 minutes. Spread the raisin bread with relish mixed with mustard. Place a hot dog in the center of each slice of raisin bread. Bring the ends of each slice of bread together and wrap with a bacon strip. Secure with toothpick. Place hot dogs on a rack in a shallow pan. Bake in a 375° oven until bacon begins to crisp, about 10 minutes—turning them just once. Serve piping hot.   *Serves 4 to 8.*

**French
Toast
Hot Dogs**

4 hot dogs
8 *slices bread*
2 *tablespoons prepared mustard*
1 *egg, beaten*
1 *tablespoon milk*
¼ *teaspoon sugar*
½ *teaspoon salt*
½ *cup cheese, grated*
Paprika

Split hot dogs, then cut in half. Spread bread with mustard. Make four sandwiches of the quartered hot dogs and bread. Beat egg in a pie plate with milk, sugar and salt. Dip sandwiches into this mixture. Set sandwiches on a greased cookie sheet. Sprinkle with grated cheese. Sprinkle paprika on each sandwich. Bake 12 minutes in a 400° oven.   *Serves 4.*

**Currant
Bake**

8 hot dogs
½ *cup currant jelly*
½ *cup prepared mustard*
½ *cup fresh lemon juice*
8 *franks*

Mix together the currant jelly, prepared mustard and fresh lemon juice. Blend until smooth. Place hot dogs on a cooky sheet. Brush heavily with currant mixture. Bake in a 375° oven for 20 minutes.   *Serves 4.*

6 hot dogs
  6 *English muffins, split and lightly toasted*
 12 *slices of fresh tomato*
  4 *teaspoons orégano*
  6 *teaspoons grated Parmesan cheese*
 12 *dill pickle slices*

Broiled Tomato Pizzas

Top each muffin half with a circle of hot dogs, cut into "pennies." Sprinkle orégano over each circle. Top each with ½ teaspoon grated cheese. Broil until heated through and cheese starts to melt, about 5 or 10 minutes. Serve with dill pickle slices.   *Serves 6.*

---

8 hot dogs
 1½ *cups shredded Cheddar cheese*
  ⅓ *cup fruit jam*
  8 *hot dog rolls*

Jamborees

Combine the cheese and jam, and blend together until smooth. Spread this cheese-jam combination on the cut surface of the bottom half of each roll. Top with a hot dog. Broil until cheese melts. Cover each hot dog with the top half of the roll, which has been toasted.   ·   *Serves 4.*

Hot Dog Hero

10 hot dogs
 6 *onions, sliced thin*
 4 *green peppers, seeded and sliced*
 ¼ *cup olive oil*
10 *midget Italian bread loaves, halved lengthwise*
 6 *tomatoes, sliced*
 1 *pound Mozzarella cheese, sliced*

Allow the sliced onions and sliced green peppers to simmer in the hot olive oil until the peppers turn limp. Be careful not to overcook or to allow the peppers to turn brown. Set aside. Place hot dogs, cut in half lengthwise, on bottoms of midget loaves, allowing two halves to a roll bottom. Top with the onion-pepper mixture. Cover with sliced tomatoes, and then with Mozzarella slices. Place under broiler until cheese turns bubbly. Meanwhile, lightly toast the tops of the midget loaves. Place a toasted loaf top on a bubbly cheesed loaf bottom until all are used, and serve. The heros will stay hot if wrapped in aluminum foil and placed in a warm oven or steam table.   *Serves 10.*

Index